# *Knocking Over*
## the Leadership Ladder

**Paul R. Ford**

St. Charles, IL 60174
1-800-253-4276

Published by ChurchSmart Resources

We are an evangelical Christian publisher committed to producing excellent products at affordable prices to help church leaders accomplish effective ministry in the areas of Church planting, Church growth, Church renewal and Leadership development.

For a free catalog of our resources call 1-800-253-4276.
Visit us at: *www.churchsmart.com*

Cover design by: Julie Becker

Manuscript edited by: Stuart Hoffman

© Copyright 2006 by Paul R. Ford

ISBN#: 1-889638-58-7

With honesty and a relentless hope for change, Paul Ford pinpoints solutions for an extreme crisis in the church: the leadership ladder. This is an issue that we must confront together. My eyes long to see the day when this ladder is knocked down.

**Dr. Bob Logan**
*CoachNet International Ministries*

If you've worked hard to get to the top and discovered that it's not all that it's cut out to be; if you are worn out from having to do all the ministry yourself; if you believe you have to be a dynamic up-front visionary to lead and you know God hasn't made you that way, this book is for you.

**Peter Drypolcher**
*Director, YWAM Frontier Missions Centre, Lusaka, Zambia*

Dr. Paul Ford has written a timely and important book. As a Christian business-person and president of a large engineering and mapping company, I have found his insight extremely valuable and applicable. In taking his words to heart I have seen personal growth in my listening skills, better understand the high priority of relationships and team building, and strive to insure that every employee plays their unique part in our organization.

**Brian Burnett**
*President, Bohannan-Huston Engineering Firm Albuquerque, NM*

If we are ever to become the dynamic, Kingdom-bringing, Body of Christ that our Heavenly Father intends and desires for us to be, this is a book which needs to be prayerfully and carefully pondered. This is a book for those that take Kingdom priorities seriously.

**Steve Weldon**
*Founding Pastor, Hope Community Church, Wichita, KS*

*Knocking Over the Leadership Ladder* reveals what Jesus values … Most of our global ministry leaders will be deeply saddened by the outcomes of their leadership and ministries when they are evaluated by Jesus. This book is a must-read for every ministry leader.

**Dr. Stacy T. Rinehart**
*International Director, MentorLink International*

# Acknowledgements

When you write about about organic functioning in the Body of Christ, it seems wise to include the Body in the process. That is what happened in *Knocking Over the Leadership Ladder*. I offer a special thanks to those friends and long-time partners in ministry who edited the contents of this book before it ever reached the publisher's hands: Kemit and Sarah Baumgardner, Nancy Boecker, Peter Drypolcher, Steve Hoke, Del Owyoung, and Emery Sauve.

And thanks also to a second group of like-minded colleagues who responded to the ideas presented in the book — my readers or "sparring partners" if you will: Bert Waggoner, Dave Bruskas, Allan Fowler, Rodney Gibson, Steven Gilbert, John Laster, Bruce Lininger, Tom Litteer, Michael Mangum, Boyd Pelley, Stacy Rinehart, Tim Roehl, Vince Rutherford, George Weinwurm, Steve Weldon, and Dick and Judy Winje.

Underlying these invaluable partners are the dear friends at ChurchSmart Resources, who consistently have given me a place to share my heart for ministry through practical resources. I thank God for the team at ChurchSmart, in particular Dave Wetzler, Bob Rummel, and graphic artist Julie Becker.

# Dedication

To Stephen James Ford

my beloved son and verbal sparring partner whose generation's response to the issues that follow will greatly affect the West's role in world evangelization.

# Table of Contents

# Foreword

This book is healing in an unexpected way.

It isn't refreshing like a weekend at a luxury spa. It goes much deeper. It is more like receiving a treatment for a severe burn. The dead skin is painfully scraped from the raw wound so that new cells may grow and heal the body. I believe you will find the concepts of leadership and body life presented in *Knocking over the Leadership Ladder* will scrape away the lifeless cells of popular man-made ideas so that the Spirit-breathed truths bring leader and follower alike new life in the context of a transformational community.

This is precisely what has happened in my life. Six months ago I was discouraged to the point of leaving a work we had planted several years earlier. I sensed I may need a new start as the point leader in a more "successful ministry" — meaning one with more people, a bigger staff and a larger budget. My wife and I gathered a prayer team around us to discern God's will. Paul and Julie Ford were two of those people. As the painful process of personal evaluation unfolded, I had concluded that not only was I ineffective in leading others spiritually, but far worse, my own spiritual life was increasingly void and dry. I was mostly frustrated because I was doing all the things I was supposed to do. I was casting vision, supervising staff, leading leaders, forming strategies, designing ministries, preaching relevant messages and, in my spare time, networking with people of influence in our city. And at the end of it all, I was discouraged, disillusioned and dry. But my greatest concern of all was for the precious people of God in this mess with me. They were raw and hurting like a severe burn on an exposed limb.

Although Dr. Ford's convictions in the pages ahead taste freshly brewed, they have percolated for years through his work training leaders representing many cultures, generations and settings. They have been the centerpiece of our lengthy and passionate discussions for the 10 years Paul has mentored me. I have always known them to be true. They are more principled than practical. They result from decades of careful and prayerful attention to Scripture. But honestly, I had only put them into practice partially. My problem with them is no different than my struggle with all of the most important truths: applying them in everyday life feels risky. The very things that bring us spiritual vitality often feel like death. Much like allowing someone to scrub an open burn wound in order to get well. But like all of God's healing truths, suffering brings joy.

If my story concluded today, it would have a happy ending. I know only six months have passed from my low point, but the transformation has a permanent feel to it. I now have a lot of "nevers" in my life. I have never had less control over ministry design and implementation. I have never been so focused on fewer relationships. I have never been more intentional in equipping and releasing people in our community. I have never seen God's people more together in serving others and reaching lost people. I have never cared less about climbing the leadership ladder. And I have never been happier....

Remember: read this book with caution. It will hurt, but it will heal.

Dave Bruskas, Lead Pastor
City on a Hill @ the Lobo Theatre
Albuquerque, New Mexico
July 17, 2006

# Introduction

Summer 2004: "Pray that our mission will not [further] succumb to believing the two big lies that pervade most large organizations: 'Anyone can be trained to do any job' and 'the best place to focus on long-term personal growth is developing your areas of weaknesses.'

These words came from a top lieutenant in one of the largest evangelical mission groups worldwide. These are great ideas, but they are not organic, biblical principles. They represent 20th and 21st century organizational management thinking about how to fulfill the task more effectively, more efficiently. What if, instead, God empowered each one specifically to fill specific parts in the body and stewardship of that design was issue one? That is, what if God already figured out what the effective strategy would be, and prepared His players accordingly? Regarding the second lie, what if God designed each of us with intrinsic, powerful strengths but also designed into each of us real weakness — so that we would automatically need others in community, those who are powerful where we are weak?

Maybe, just maybe, there are times that we are not as helpful to God with our strategies as we sometimes like to think.

Summer 2005: "I sat in a 'Lead Like Jesus' seminar. You are probably familiar with it. Anyway, the first part of it is good because it deals with the heart, but then they move right into the same old visionary leader stuff that everybody's supposed to be whether it's as a CEO (Chief Executive Officer), a missionary, or a parent. It made me think of you, Paul. Its biggest weakness, as with all of U.S. evangelical Christianity, is that it said NOTHING about the church, about spiritual gifts or community. So, I guess we can lead like Jesus, but we don't have to do it in his Body!"

This comment came from the heart of another large mission group having impact in every region of the world — again from a top lieutenant in the trenches on the field.

Wait a minute.

What if God prepared the body of Christ to adapt to situations and then brought His sovereignly-prepared players to the right situations at the right time with the needed spiritual gifts and passions? It certainly would make God look smart, eh?

A funny thing happened on the way to mobilizing the laity in the body of Christ 15 years ago. I took cross-cultural, teambuilding and leadership detours along the way and discovered something for which I was not looking. Guess what I found? We have a ladder in the West that everyone is supposed to climb and the impact is everywhere. Business and management cultures in the West have influenced how we build and lead our Christian organizations and the resulting impact has changed the way we see the tasks, processes, and results of our Kingdom work.

We have a climbing disease — and the source of this problem has caught me by surprise. You see, I found out twelve years ago that I was climbing the ladder of success and significance in my own life — and I have found thousands just like me since. In fact, after fifteen years of working across the body of Christ in the United States and actively training leaders and teams in eight other cultures worldwide, I have found a strong enemy foothold in a place where I did not expect to find it — in my own culture. Bigger is better, more is better, higher is better. Great idea ... it just is not how God designed His body and His players to work. And in some places, it's wreaking havoc to major proportions, breaking leaders, teams, churches and mission groups everywhere in our culture. And now it is affecting other cultures as we export our strategies in sharing the Gospel worldwide.

What brought me to the conclusions that I will be sharing with you? There are at least four myths that have led to our U.S. evangelical dilemma. I will start there. And, as we address the four myths, I will counter with four biblical realities. I will offer clear biblical alternatives to stand against the mythical world enabled by the evil one to mislead us — or, rather, to still, kill and destroy us.

After we consider these myths and the alternative biblical realities, the second major section will consider a new wineskin that is as old as Jesus' resurrection and the coming of the Holy Spirit in power. The proverbial ladder cannot stand when faced with such organic dynamics as the Holy Spirit can release. We will look at the new model and its impact on leaders, teams and whole ministries.

The last major section will bring life to those Ezekial 37 bones through specific wineskins in which we can carry the new wine. While I don't expect anyone to follow the whole of what I suggest, your present paradigms will be greatly shaken — or at least challenged to consider new attitudes, values and action!

Over the past 20 years, after working with over 15,000 Christians who function in some form of oversight or ministry management, one thing is certain just now: everyone wants to be a leader. The problem? Few know what a Christian leader really is. They just know they have to be one.

In reviewing a number of leadership definitions, multiple attempts from many resources talked about leadership as personality or style or influence or positional power or gifts or making decisions or vision sharing or looking out the window or managing or empowering others — or some or all of the aforementioned. And this is before we get to folks who define leadership more by the results attained. And the baby builders generation and the baby boomers generation and the baby busters generation all seem to have a different take on this. My, this IS confusing.

There are problems in this leadership lair. For example, I really like the "looking out the window to see the vision" idea, except that seven out of ten leaders with whom I work cannot find the window (i.e. cannot find the vision on their own!!).

To limit confusion, throughout my book I will function with a definition of leadership that looks like, ... wait. No, I'm not going to do it. Please read John Maxwell or George Barna, or Max DePree or somebody else for that. I plan to walk you through the organizational battlefield created amidst this leadership dilemma and then bring the new wine and new wineskins to the rescue. I will give you a definition of leadership at just the right time. You may not change your use of leadership language but you will have a chance to consider clearly the many issues in play because of the "L" word.

Maybe, just maybe, leadership is not the issue for Christians in equipping roles throughout the Kingdom of God, including the United States of America. Let's take a look together.

Paul Ford

# SECTION I

## Stale Wine and Cracked Wineskins

For twelve years I have been watching the evangelical Christian subculture in the United States from an unusual vantage point. Three or four times a year, I travel to any of eight different cultures in places like Russia, Kazakhstan (in central Asia), Korea, Malaysia and Zimbabwe. Consider me an observant ping-pong ball: back and forth, back and forth, and back and forth. After several years of coming home from my overseas trips, I observed a number of unmistakable lifestyle patterns developing in the West that concerned me. These disturbing trends appeared to already have a firm foothold in my own evangelical Christian subculture. Actually, the patterns were already there by the time I began watching in the mid-nineties, but I suddenly saw more clearly what was happening in my own world at home. I also found myself weeping at what I observed.

I identified at least four distinct myths that encouraged an upwardly mobile movement in Christian approaches to life and ministry as related to leadership. As I describe each myth in these first three chapters, I contrast the cultural myth with the biblical reality to which we are called as disciples of Jesus.

Myth #1  The Christian Leadership Myth Versus
the Biblical Reality of the Equipping Releaser

Myth #2  The Individualism Myth (Build Me) Versus
the Biblical Reality of the Community

Myth #3  The Ladder Myth (Build Me UP) Versus
the Biblical Reality of Stewardship

**Myth #4    The Sarcasm Myth (Put You DOWN)** Versus
**the Biblical Reality of Encouragement**

The biblical reality of leadership does not live on a ladder — it does not even own a ladder!

# CHAPTER ONE

## Christian Leadership Versus the Equipping Releaser

I now become myself.
It's taken time, many years and places.
I have been dissolved and shaken,
Worn other people's faces [1]

You are not certain what leadership is. But in this day and age, you somehow feel that you have to be a leader — and moving up. Welcome to the leadership myth.

In my early Christian growth years, Tim was the person that I wanted to emulate. He was a charismatic leader. People flocked to him. He could say the right thing and inspire people with a clear vision — both at the same time. It seemed that people would follow him anywhere. He was a pied piper who could play the tune in such a way that people would step out and come along for the journey.

That was for me! I wanted to lead just like that. We will put aside, for the moment, that my pursuit at that point was partly my own search for significance. I knew — or thought I knew — that leading like Tim would make me a leader after God's own heart, with the throngs following my every word. The charismatic, inspirational leader was the model for me. But I soon discovered that I was a poor copy of Tim; I just could not pull it off. It did not work for me. I made a very poor Tim.

As it turned out, I was somewhat ahead of the crowd in my desire to live out that leadership myth in the late 1970's. With the growth of the visionary leader model in the West over the past 25 years, it seems that now everybody wants to be like Tim! Everyone wants to be a visionary leader, a leader who has influence over others in some tangible way. Somewhere, somehow, the message became, "Move up, become more important." Everyone could move from good to great.

As a spiritual gifts specialist, I have noticed an interesting shift in people's perceptions of their gifts that has developed over the past twenty years. In the early years of gifts-mobilizing seminars in the mid-eighties, the most-desired gift evangelical and main-line Christians did not have but projected having in their gifts questionnaires was the gift of teaching. The projected gift of choice in the charismatic/pentecostal world was the gift of prophecy. By the early 1990's, an intriguing thing happened. A new gift hit the top of the charts! The gift most coveted in each of these Christian arenas suddenly became the gift of leadership.

The new king of the spiritual gifts hill was crowned. Charismatics and pentecostals still wanted to be apostles and prophets, even as the "third wave" movement broke onto the scene. But the gift of leadership was taking its turn in the sun even then. As represented in gifts survey results, people were moving toward a new understanding of spiritual leadership. And that new world was driven by the gift of leadership, a place where everyone would need to climb to find his or her place in the sun. Moving up became vogue.

How did this happen? How did this myth come about and begin affecting all Christians?

## Traces of the Leadership Myth

So you want to make something of your life? The smart money says, Become a leader. I have observed evidence of this "leadership myth" in at least six different aspects of life and ministry:

**1.) The Business World.** In addition to gaining insights from traveling back and forth between cultures, I also read business literature, including such periodicals as *Business Week, Inc.* and *Fast Company.* While I worked for the Charles Fuller Institute of Evangelism and Church Growth (CEFI) back in the early nineties, I noted something of great interest. At that time CEFI, a Christian leadership niche publisher, was seeking to "redeem business principles for the Kingdom of God." Simply stated, there is much in the business world from which the church can learn, and we can even adapt some of those organizational principles and use them to build the kingdom of God. My association with CEFI alerted me to the best business books I read in those days.

One generalization purported in the nineties, and still central for many in today's business literature, is that anyone can be a leader in business — for that matter, in organizational management at any level. Consider this recent quote from Kouzes and Posner in *The Leadership Challenge:* "These [leadership] practices aren't the property of the people we studied or of a few select shining stars. They are available to anyone, in any organization or situation, who accepts the leadership challenge."[2]

The message people hear is that anyone who wants to become a strong leader simply needs to "...accept the leadership challenge..." and learn to effectively carry out the leadership activities in Kouzes and Posner's

> **To be a leader — or attain leadership — is a goal of highest value today.**

model. I have recently observed several friends — both in ministry and workplace settings — use this book for exactly that purpose. Kouzes and Posner write much more on this subject in other books; they actually do *not* believe that everyone can be a leader. Yet many are grabbing that initial message and running with it. To be a leader — or attain leadership — is a goal of highest value today.

While the purpose of this book is not to challenge secular organizational and management sages, I do have some obvious concerns about the overall truth of this principle in the business world. As a leadership and teambuilding specialist utilizing *The Birkman Method*, a sophisticated personality profiling tool[3], I have spent time consulting with at least one business client monthly over the past seven years. This has given me an ongoing laboratory to check out this theory. I have sincere concern about the unrealistic expectations placed on many by the belief that anyone can be a leader. But, since our focus is the Christian leader, suffice to say that this organizational principle has, without question, had an effect on the Christian approach to leadership development.

During my days at The Fuller Institute, I saw the overlap between business and Christian management concepts become indistinguishable in certain areas, the most obvious being this leadership development category. I noticed various seminar outlines used during those years had major sections that gave credit to secular leadership development and business management books. I also participated in several projects in the late nineties with a group called Leadership Network and was a presenter at their lay mobilization national conferences at the turn of the century. During that time, the influence of the late sociologist and business guru Peter Drucker on that organization was unmistakable, as was the mission to help large churches become more effective organizationally.

Was there anything wrong or mythical with that? Not necessarily, as much of the influence brought to the church and mission world from such principles has brought about some better administrative processes and thus healthier organizations. And it is certainly feasible that, in the everyday, secular world of organizations, people can learn skills that can make them more effective in their work.

**2.) The Overlay Between the Business and Christian Worlds.** As I noted, I am a habitual reader of *Business Week*. I read it because everything in the West today is driven by economics. What better place to watch U.S. and worldwide trends than through such a weekly publication? A recent article brought to light an important reality in discovering the heart of the leadership myth: *any Christian can become a leader.*

This feature story was titled "Earthly Kingdoms: How Evangelical Churches are Borrowing from the Business Playbook." As a reader of *Business Week* for many years, I had seen many articles on the new buying power of the evangelical subculture. Numerous articles over the years had traced the growing influence of conservative Christianity in politics, evidenced in the George W. Bush presidential victories – often credited to the "religious right."

But this article was different. Suddenly, the "white evangelical church," now 26% of the Christian market in the U.S. according to the article[4], was being discussed in ways very similar to a growing corporation. One might think that the evangelical church, in its own right, has become another player in the world of politics, business, and finance, and should be treated as such. Here are some excerpts:

> Their [evangelical entrepreneurs] runaway success is modeled unabashedly on business. They borrow tools ranging from niche marketing to MBA [Masters in Business Administration] hiring to lift their share of U.S. churchgoers.
>
> Many evangelical pastors focus intently on a huge market potential. ... So successful are some that they're opening up branches like so many Home Depots or Subways. ... Branding whizzes that they are, the new church leaders are spreading their ideas through every available outlet.
>
> Evangelicals' eager embrace of corporate style growth strategies is giving them tremendous advantage in the battle for religious market share. [5]

Wait a minute. "Market share"?

First, let me express my excitement about our evangelistic approaches aimed at reaching unbelievers in definable groups through the use of niche-market strategies. In this I am really encouraged! We are learning to understand and initially meet unbelievers through their frame of reference, rather than demanding them to come to us. That is, we are seeking them out in their world and seeking common ground through which to draw them to the Lord and not expecting them to always come seeking through our church doors.

However, the article does create a new set of questions for us. Are we now so much a part of our secular world that we are praised for our secular marketing techniques? Have we become so much like our world that they see us as going after "market share" like the rest of the corporate world? I highlight this article to reveal the significant overlap between evangelicals and the business world. And, given such overlap, we must be careful not to buy in to the ways of business and organizational management strategies simply because they appear to work.

As we bear in mind the focus of this book, what about the area of leadership development? What if we have bought in to the business model at a level beyond what is healthy and we are no longer able to discriminate between what is godly and what is worldly? What if, in fact, we actually have begun to think we can help God fulfill his purposes with our great strategies?

We must reflect on such questions as the church decides what its identity should be — what God wants it to be. In a note to me, Danny Sims, a friend in ministry, traced the history of the church's identity: "When the church was headquartered in Jerusalem, she was a fellowship. In the early Pauline years we see Athens and Greece as the 'thought center' of the church where she became a philosophy. Then the church had its center in Rome and became an institution. Then it radically affected Northern Europe where she became a culture. Now, in the United States, she is becoming an enterprise."[6]

## Anyone Can Be a Christian Leader

**3.) Christian Literature on Leadership.** From business literature in the secular world we move to Christian literature and to primary sources for the Christian leadership myth. Christian leadership often differs from organizational management in areas of motivation, values, and desired outcomes. But, as we have seen already, principles can carry over from the secular to the Christian world. In fact, in the early nineties evangelical books on leadership began promoting the notion that anyone can be a leader.

As early as 1993 John Maxwell, then senior pastor of Skyline Wesleyan Church in San Diego, California, made clear statements about this:

> Leadership is not an exclusive club for those who were "born with it." The traits that are the raw materials of leadership can be acquired. Link up with them with desire and nothing can keep you from becoming a leader.... You must supply the desire....
>
> To stay on top, natural leadership characteristics must be developed. ... I have discovered that they all fit into four categories or levels of leadership. [7]

It is here that we turn a mythical corner where the secular tries to become Christian. However, much of the evangelical world has not seemed to notice either the origin of the myth or its fallacy. In fact, many Christian leaders have begun the climb up the leadership ladder or have sought to position themselves as valued, influential leaders.

We were told that everyone can become a leader. That is, everyone can move up the ladder as it relates to serving in the kingdom of God. As in the secular business world, where people are trained to move up in their organization, so the model becomes a part of the Christian leadership development process. The church growth movement of the late seventies and eighties certainly played into this business design. According to C. Peter Wagner, the American church growth guru and one of my early mentors, healthy churches are to grow and those churches need healthy, growth-minded leaders [8]. Mega-churches were growing up to prominence, and their quality leaders were coming to the fore, for example, John Maxwell at Skyline, Bill Hybels at Willow Creek Church in suburban Chicago, and Rick Warren at Saddleback Church in southern Orange County, California. Growing churches need strong leaders who are themselves growing.

During the late seventies into the eighties and early nineties, this became a common focus for many pastors. The church growth movement was a major player in the drive for healthy, growing churches. The theme question for nearly two decades was, "How can I become such a leader — or prove that I am a leader who can grow a church?" The soil was fertile for leaders to be the ones who set a clear course.

George Barna, in his 1992 book *The Power of Vision*, unwittingly strengthened and sharpened this leader mindset with his detailed discussion of the Christian leader as visionary. While providing an excellent overview of the role of vision in the life of a church and its leader, he affirms that every leader fundamentally needs to be a visionary: "By definition, all leaders are visionaries."[9] His hope certainly was to affirm the importance of a pastor or leader's need to work hard on discerning God's vision and then communicate it, that is, to be that visionary leader. "Similarly, a common characteristic of all true leaders is that they have vision. A godly leader is one who operates from a base of God's vision for his or her ministry."[10] This took an already sharp edge — that everyone can be a leader — and sharpened it even more by adding "visionary" to the essence of what that leader should be by design.

Unfortunately, this sharpening cuts both ways. As I began to work with pastors during this time, I was overwhelmed by the numbers who were convinced that God had called them to grow a church and become a visionary leader. However, I was troubled from the start as I also found in many of these pastors a nagging sense of guilt commonly growing in tandem with the felt need to become the visionary leader of such growth in their church or mission. The pressure on the average pastor to succeed increased as vision became the new savior and the new pressure cooker.

Let us stop and consider the context in which this exciting church growth and leadership movement language was being publicized. The older pastors hearing this message from Maxwell, Wagner, Barna, and others, were men (mostly) and women who had been trained in a more traditional model where the leader of the church was the pastor. That is, the emphasis was not on leading the flock so much as caring for or tending the sheep. "Pastor" was the role, and a variety of gifts, including pastoring, exhortation, teaching, and leadership, were common among pastors who would shepherd their flocks. My grandfather, schooled in the early 1900's, and my father, trained in the 1940's, were emblematic of this training. My grandfather actually functioned as an evangelist in his ministry, but the role of pastor — of flock tending — still dominated even a man with a "soul-winning" gift.

In the midst of my father's ministry, especially the 1960's and beyond, the gift of teaching rose up alongside the shepherding role. There were great teaching-style preachers from a breadth of theological backgrounds — James Boice, John MacArthur, and C.M. Ward — and seminar teachers like Bill Gothard. These strong teachers, plus the growth of the Christian education movement in general, brought even greater prominence to the gift of teaching. The classic pastor often was a "pastor-teacher," one who not only tended the flock but also protected it from wolves who would bring in false doctrine. As I have watched spiritual gifting in Christian leadership over 20 years, I have been greatly intrigued that the most common gift combination in pastors of churches under 150 in attendance is the pastor-teacher combination. We have the hint here of something that may reveal a portion of God's organic design. Perhaps God provides what is needed gift-wise in every situation, and such is the primary need in the spiritual leadership of churches this size: tender care and protection of the flock.

As the church growth movement grew and the "leadership ladder" movement took root, there were still pastors and missionaries who were the older, traditional shepherds as well as some who modeled great Bible teaching. During this time in the parachurch world, there were also several powerful evangelistic ministries arising from such people as Billy Graham and Campus Crusade's Bill Bright. These ministries gave prominence to the spiritual gift of evangelism.

Thus, from a gifts standpoint, the pattern moved from pastoring to teaching, followed by the rise of evangelism from the parachurch arena, and then finally to the rise of the leadership gift. Unfortunately, my work alongside 70-plus different denominational and mission groups revealed that with this last development, the number of guilt-ridden pastors and missionaries grew dramatically! The leadership gift and the visionary leader concept became the in vogue way of climbing the leadership ladder for the evangelical pastor. We are now dealing with the results of this perceived spiritual "upward mobility" (to be analyzed at greater depth in chapter 3).

In my first ten years of working with churches, missions, and their respective leadership, I determined that, on average, two or three out of ten leaders had the true gift of leadership. That is, two or three were able, among other things, to originate vision from the Lord on their own without anxiety or dismay. Five of the ten, while not able to discover the vision from God, were able to clearly communicate vision with equipping spiritual gifts other than the gift of leadership. That left two or three whose gifts were not gifts that could discover or communicate vision of any kind. That is, they were fish out of water, perhaps misplaced in a leadership role.

One moving illustration on this issue comes from the idea of the leader seeking a vision from God. The leader needs to take time to think and pray about the personal vision God had prepared for that leader in his or her respective church or ministry. The image of "looking out the window" became a common word picture for this. As I talked about leaders searching for God's vision, I would illustrate the statistics in the previous paragraph in this way. Two or three leaders are able to catch God's vision as they look out the window — but the other seven have a problem. They cannot even find the window! Put simply, they are lost in the vision discovery process. Because of this struggle, the resultant guilt for most became a serious issue. Therein lay a major portion of my concern: If you glorify one gift, especially a gift you do not have, such internal tyranny will be a part of the fruit of seeking that gift.

> **If you glorify one gift, especially a gift you do not have, such internal tyranny will be a part of the fruit of seeking that gift.**

So then, while Barna hoped for more leaders to step up as visionary leaders, I considered the realities facing the body of Christ in America. With only a maximum of three pastors in ten at present (Barna's numbers were lower than mine) who meet the criteria of a visionary leader, what are we to do?

My response is simple: Either God really messed up, or there is another way that he has designed the kingdom model of organic body life to work.

> **Either God really messed up, or there is another way that he has designed the kingdom model of organic body life to work.**

**4.) Team Building Seminars.** After stepping out of local church ministry and into a broader training ministry with Church Resource Ministries in 1992, I began to do team-building seminars with leadership teams from local churches and mission agencies. From the beginning, a pattern emerged that confirmed this leadership myth playing itself out, something I have found consistently true in over 200 team-building events, in all sizes and shapes of groups, in different theologies, and across scores of denominations and missions.

In all team-building seminars my participants will have completed a gift assessment in either my *Discovering Your Ministry Identity* workbook or the *Your Leadership Grip* workbook.[11] For the sake of discussion, we will use ten people as the average size of a team with which I work. Commonly, I find that six to eight of the ten people in the room claim that they have the spiritual gift of leadership.

However, consider the incredible design complexities of the body of

Christ. Note Romans 12:4-6: "Just as each of us has one body with many members, and these members do not all have the same function, so in Christ we who are many form one body, and each member belongs to all the others. We have different gifts, according to the grace given us." Each person has different gifts, and certainly a broad range of gifts is endowed to a given group in any given location. Consider the odds of any one group where seven people all have the same spiritual gift. Further, note that the common gift perceived by groups in team-building or training events is always — repeat, *always* — the gift of leadership! I can recall only one occasion when another gift dominated in a similar way — the gift of exhortation. In charismatic or pentecostal settings, frequently three or four out of ten believe they are prophets. However, even in these settings the gift of leadership is consistently the dominant spiritual gift projected by people.

Here is how I address this phenomenon in team-building events. During the seminar, I say something along these lines: "Let's consider the fact that you are all leaders functioning in leadership roles. Tag, you're it. You *are* a leader. Now then, let us figure out *how* you lead." That takes the heat off each individual, and normally by the end of our two or three days together, only two or maybe three believe they have the gift of leadership. The others say something like this: "I lead power-fully using these equipping spiritual gifts." By changing the focus to function and away from having to validate oneself as a leader through the leadership gift, we came closer to discerning real gifting for each person.

Clearly, many Christians in ministry are so concerned about being perceived as a leader that they commonly project having that gift to prove what they hope to be true.

**5.) Leaders Searching for Their Identity.** I saw the pattern first in secular business literature and then noticed it develop within the evangelical Christian leadership world of church growth and church planting. I saw whole organizations attempt to train people to do the same activity the same way across the board, believing that all would achieve the same results because they were trained similarly. I saw hundreds of players on their respective teams project the spiritual gift of leadership because it somehow seemed to make them better, more important, more strategic, or perhaps higher on a ladder.

Recently, I also had a window to observe some trends related to this leadership myth among individual Christian leaders. For four years I taught a doctoral course to evangelical pastors at a seminary on the West Coast. Each of the 80 students I worked with had to write an 18 to 20 page summary paper on "The Stewardship of Who I Am." There were three parts to the summary: 1.) From the *Discovering Your Ministry Identity* workbook results, describe your ministry identity — that is, who you are in Christ; 2.) compare and contrast how your ministry identity fits with your current role; and 3.) determine a plan of action that will bring more intentional stewardship of who you are into your present and future ministry.

Shockingly, one of the consistent issues addressed in the first and second sections of the papers — between 70% and 75% of the group — was a sadness or disappointment for not being the kind of "great leader" they had believed they would become. Here is a representative quote from one of the pastors:

> This leadership "failure" has been an important part of my transition to a new phase of life. It has caused me to wonder about my ability to reach what I believe to be my potential. It has caused me to reflect on my ministry focus. It has caused me to wrestle with God over the issue of ambition [the leadership ladder] and purpose. [12]

In spite of apparent impact and fruitful ministry among the majority of those who wrote about their ministry experience, there was clearly a sense of not having "climbed high enough" in their leadership roles positionally. And, in the majority of the papers where I found this expressed, the third section included a resetting of focus to become a more intentional steward of who they are in Christ rather than trying to be or do something that no longer relates to their understanding of their respective ministry identities. For several whose gifts were all supporting gifts, they suddenly understood why they never found a meaningful fit in primary spiritual leadership.

**6.) Spiritual Gifts Classes.** From 1987-1992, I worked with a team of laypersons to develop an extremely effective lay mobilizing process called "Discovering and Using Your Spiritual Gifts," a process still having impact in many churches to this day.[13] As one of several facilitators, I taught a part of the material where we distinguished between equipping gifts and supporting gifts. (These terms are more fully defined in chapter 6.) Students tended to associate equipping gifts with leadership, and supporting gifts with more behind-the-scenes roles.

As we talked about who people are from a spiritual gifts standpoint, I confirmed that people could have only equipping gifts, only supporting gifts, or a combination of the two. Within that teaching, one important concept we emphasized was this: people whose gifts are all supporting gifts *cannot* lead powerfully. It is part of God's design and his plan!

Regardless of whether you agree or disagree with our rationale, consider the result of offering this insight in our mobilizing class teaching. Every quarterly class for five years, at least one person came up to me privately, usually weeping. They would say something like, "I have all supporting gifts. Thank you for validating me as a Christian for the first time in my Christian life." I soon came to realize that the leadership myth is so strong in the U.S. that people with supporting spiritual gifts experience a tremendous devaluing in the body of Christ.

> **The leadership myth is so strong in the U.S. that people with supporting spiritual gifts experience a tremendous devaluing in the body of Christ.**

Amazingly, I have found the same pattern in every cultural setting in which I have ministered — now over one hundred ministries in fifteen different cultures worldwide. I will never forget the first time I shared this in cross-cultural training in the former Soviet republic of Kazakhstan in Central Asia. Five Russians came running to me during the first break after hearing this content, several in tears. One said "I have found freedom now in using the gifts I do have ... supporting gifts!" Another said, "Now I know why I was so frustrated and why I never felt comfortable functioning in leadership roles. I was designed by God to support and not lead. I am free!"

We should be seriously concerned about a model that says everyone can be a leader. Our concern is especially important in a cultural context where upward mobility is glorified, where more power or more education or a "higher" position is always perceived to be better. When people feel unduly driven to be leaders, they can become captive to an unhealthy situation.

The "everyone can be a leader" training model is not the only unhealthy model. Another occurs when an organization focuses on one primary task to fulfill its overall mission. It may determine one skill-set that is most effective in fulfilling that task. Rather than train everyone to be leaders, the organization may train them to all be, say, evangelists.

In training leaders and teams throughout the body of Christ, I have found several large ministry organizations that have done this very thing. The overall influence of one such group is great in many parts of the world, but underneath the amazing impact and results I have found many people who have actually left the organization as broken or angry people. Their common responses, "I cannot be who they want me to be." The "one size fits all" approach created an internal tension that caused people to either try hard to be something that, by God's design, they could not be — and thus deal with tremendous internal tension — or they left the organization. People cannot be trained to be someone whom they are not. God designed people to be just who he wanted them to be, so we must indeed be careful to free people to be that powerful, God-designed player. Training and the related accountability to do or be something outside of people's giftedness, at best, leads to guilt in their resulting ineffectiveness and powerlessness.

In summary, I am convinced that the majority of us who minister in the evangelical Christian subculture in the United States are internally and externally motivated to see ourselves as leaders who are somehow moving upward, somehow "successful," and somehow leaders — more than anything else, leaders. There's something magical about that word. If you have only supporting spiritual gifts, you may not "have what it takes" in your culture.

My response is simple: either God really messed up by designing people to be supernaturally endowed with a range of gifts other than leadership, or there is another way that he has designed his model, the body of Christ, to work.

Many have said that we need more leaders in the Church. However, perhaps what we need is a different paradigm.

## The Equipping Releaser and its Biblical Reality

If it is not about leadership, then what is the story line supposed to be for pastors, missionaries, and other leaders in the Christian world? The myth is that every Christian can be a leader. Compounding this myth is another that every real leader should be a visionary leader. The anti-myth, the biblical reality, is that God has prepared some Christians to be "equipping releasers" of others.

We start with language from Ephesians 4:12, where equippers in the body of Christ prepare, train, or mend others to play their God-designed roles in kingdom service. Those who are over others in the Lord[14] have a clear-cut responsibility to function with spiritual gifts that have an equipping function, of which the gift of leadership is one. Actually, there is nothing wrong with leadership or the gift of leadership. However, a conceptual reversal has taken place.

Historically, the leadership gift was a subset of the larger group of equipping gifts that God has given so that the whole body of players can be prepared, mentored, or trained for their God-designed role. However, the equipping gifts have become a subset of leadership. More clearly stated, gifts like evangelism, exhortation, pastor and prophet are now subservient to the leader concept and the leadership gift. Whatever your gifts, it is all about leadership.

What should we do in response to this reversal? We need to knock over the ladder that has been propping up the leadership gift and its broader application! Let's move the leadership gift back into its proper place, as one of the valuable equipping spiritual gifts that are used powerfully for kingdom-building purposes. God gave multiple types of equipping gifts because different functions are needed to equip and release others in the varying contexts of life and ministry. How wise God is!

Leaders in the body of Christ may have the gift of leadership, or they may have a combination of other gifts through which they can powerfully lead or enable this process of equipping and releasing the saints for the work of ministry. Christians must not seek the position or the gift of leadership; rather they must seek to empower others to discover and fulfill their places in the body. Our pursuit of leadership does not put us in any higher or lower status. The kingdom of God is not about position, but about stewardship of how God has prepared each of us to play our parts.

One phrase that has always struck me when leadership is discussed in evangelical circles is "Moses as CEO" (Chief Executive Officer). People identify with Moses' strength of conviction, with his acceptance of the call to lead his people, and with his clarity of vision. Add to that his execution of an effective exit strategy out of Egypt with thousands of people, and you have the model of a great leader.

What has struck me most, though, about Moses as CEO, is that he did not become the true CEO until he understood equipping and releasing! Though he was directly in the presence of God on several occasions, and came away with a radiant face at one point, he still struggled with the role of executive oversight of all the tasks in the growth of corporate Israel. Not until Exodus 18 do we see his transformation into true executive leadership. Jethro, Moses' father-in-law, observes Moses serving as the sole judge for all the people from morning until night. He asks Moses why it is this way. Many Christian leaders have problems similar to that of Moses in sharing ministry responsibilities. They can draw a powerful lesson from this passage:

> Moses answered him, "Because the people come to me to seek God's will. Whenever they have a dispute, it is brought to me, and I decide between the parties and inform them of God's decrees and laws." Moses' father-in-law replied, "What you are doing is not good. You and these people who come to you will only wear yourselves out. The work is too heavy for you; you cannot handle it alone. ... Select capable men from all the people — men who fear God, trustworthy men who hate dishonest gain — and appoint them as officials over thousands, hundreds, fifties, and tens. Have them serve as judges for the people at all times, but have them bring every difficult case to you." ... Moses listened to his father-in-law and did everything he said. [15]

Have you ever stopped to wonder why there is so little focus on the concept of leadership in the Old and New Testaments? If not, begin the wonderment now. God has prepared some new wine for the New Millennium, found in the old winecellar of Scripture.

## Endnotes for Chapter 1

[1] Sarton, May. *Collected Poems* (NY: Norton, 1974), p. 156

[2] Kouzes, James M. & Posner, Barry Z, *The Leadership Challenge, Third Edition* (San Francisco: Jossey-Bass, 2002), p 13.

[3] *www.birkman.com*

[4] Symonds, William C. Earthly Empires: "How Evangelical Churches Are Borrowing from the Business Playbook," *Business Week*, May 23, 2005 p. 80, 84.

[5] Ibid, p 80-84

[6] Sims, Danny. Personal notes.

[7] Maxwell, John. *Developing the Leader Within You* (Nashville: Thomas Nelson Publishers, 1993), Introduction.

[8] Wagner, C. Peter. *Your Church Can Grow* (1976).

[9] Barna, George. *The Power of Vision* (Ventura, CA: Regal Books, 1992), p 47.

[10] Ibid.

[11] *Discovering Your Ministry Identity* workbook assesses six areas that affect how people function on a team, and *Your Ministry Identity* is a self-discovery assessment process focused exclusively on identifying the leader's spiritual gifts from three different angles. Both are available through ChurchSmart Resources, 800-253-4276 or *www.churchsmart.com*.

[12] Anonymous Fuller Seminary doctoral student, "The Stewardship of Who I Am" paper, p 2.

[13] Now called the "Mobilizing Spiritual Gifts Series," this set of resources is available through ChurchSmart Resources, 800-253-4276 or *www.churchsmart.com*.

[14] 1 Thessalonians 5:12.

[15] Exodus 18: 15-24.

# CHAPTER TWO

## Build ME Versus
## Build Community

I walk a lonely road,
The only one I have ever known;
Don't know where it goes,
But it's only me and I walk alone.

My shadow's the only one that walks beside me;
My shallow heart's the only one thing that's beating.
Sometimes I wish someone up there will find me;
    'til then I walk alone.

**"Boulevard of Broken Dreams"** Green Day rock group

People of the postmodern era deeply desire to find real community. The breakdown of the family; the boomer drive for success and material gain, often at the forfeit of relational investment; and the growing depersonalization of so many American systems — all have fed this sincere desire for authentic community.

Believing this to be true, I went to one of the new world communities: the cyberspace chat room. I noticed some very interesting dynamics in this world. People, many who fit this profile of desiring real community out of their own brokenness, often use a fake name and often distort facts about themselves to find acceptance. They may even be vulnerable about real need, confess intimate weakness or hurt, yet still hold out on their real name and true identity. Note that such an approach to community has a distinctively individualistic bent, more focused on "myself" and "my needs" than "ourselves" and "our needs."

Then, I looked to another new cultural reality as a source for the postmodern community about which I had heard. In the nineties virtual teams were a hot commodity. You could be a real team without even living in the same place! A group of people, using the amazing communication capacities of the Internet and conference calling, could corporately fulfill their mission "virtually." Tasks got done, strategic movement took place, and you got results. All of this happened but you did not have to live in the same place to see, feel, and sense each other face to face. My own mission group got excited about this because it provided a way to complete missional tasks even though team members were spread throughout the country. In many cases, though, groups only got halfway to being "virtual teams." They were practical and effective as the word *virtual* implies, but the team part — the relational part — was often left wanting.

In fact, I have discovered one consistent and serious problem with virtual teams. In many ways they are not teams! They are task groups and working groups, where the individuals each complete their parts of the overall mission. But in the process, deeper relationships and a cohesive unity seldom happen. My definition of *team* includes a sense of belonging that grows out of the interaction and sharing together in owning the vision and sharing in the tasks. For many virtual teams, finding a unity of purpose or relationship beyond the task was just too tall an order from a distance. It is difficult to go deeper relationally when contact does not include regular eye contact — or heart contact, where you see and feel and sense with people alongside you in the flesh. But in a culture that is more individually than community oriented, virtual teams fulfill the task — which for many is enough.

> **I have discovered one consistent and serious problem with virtual teams. In many ways they are not teams!**

The search for community in our Western postmodern world is, unquestionably, both real and pervasive. But just because people want community does not mean that their approaches to finding greater unity and purpose in relationships, or fulfilling important tasks together, will bring intimacy or any sense of real community. More specifically, in the evangelical Christian world, when the focus on community in team or small group life does not move beyond the wants, needs, or task fulfillment of the individual, it is extremely difficult to build a depth of lasting unity in relationships.

> **Put simply, it is difficult to find the communion of the Holy Spirit when the spotlight is on the self.**

Put simply, it is difficult to find the communion of the Holy Spirit when the spotlight is on the self. The influence of individualism and all that it promises are evident in many sub-cultures in the postmodern United States.

## It's All About Me

*Business Week* helped show me what was happening in my own culture. The June 1997 cover article on advertising was highly enlightening. The focal question was, "Have we gone too far in advertising to children?" Remember, this was *Business Week*, not *Christianity Today*. The article pointed out the changing role between parents and their children: "Parents no longer act as filters between their kids and the outside world."[1] Peers and advertising were both seen as influences greater than parents, certainly still true today.

**Narcissism, Entitlement, and Dissatisfaction.** The article's most disturbing quote was this: "The combination of 400 ads a day creates in children a combination of narcissism, entitlement, and dissatisfaction."[2] A Church of Christ elder in the Southwest commented in 1998: "I don't know why you are making such a big deal out of those three words — narcissism, entitlement, and dissatisfaction. They are just Marketing Strategy 101." I was stunned.

If this is true of our children, and we are somewhere between one and two decades past the beginning of such pervasive advertising, what is the result? What happens in a culture where content that actively encourages narcissism, entitlement, and dissatisfaction is constantly on the television, on the radio, on the billboards, and now in the schools? Let's stop and look at this phenomenon of individualism as seen through the article's words.

To understand *narcissism*, let us look at the origin. Narcissus was a figure in Greek mythology who looked in a pool of water, and, caught by the beauty of the reflection seen, fell in love with himself.[3] The psychological term *narcissism* comes from this character, who became so captivated with himself that he fell into the water and drowned! Narcissism, exaggerated self-concern, says, "It is all about me. I am the center of my universe. What I want is what is most important, since it is all about me."

Where do we see narcissisism in our culture? Consider this quote from a team-building consultant in the business world attempting to grasp one corporation's team identity:

> The concept of aligning a disparate group of individuals for the good of the company is undergoing a 21st century makeover, as an avalanche of books, speakers, and coaching programs shifts attention away from the "team" and toward the individual and his or her pursuit of individual satisfaction. I spent ten years of looking at organizational change, and what I found was that I didn't have one organization, but I had 3500 different worlds that just happened to collide between nine and five.[4]

The subtitle of this article provided another clue as to the challenge teams face in this 21st century individualism: "Forget teambuilding and bonding. Experts say catering to the individual employees' personal desires yields far more productivity."[5] It is for such reasons that, when doing team-building seminars in America with Christian leadership teams, I offer this definition of an American team, Christian or otherwise: "a group of people who happen to be in the same place at the same time, each doing his or her own thing." If we were voting, you could say that the I's have it.

What if narcissism is extended to its logical extreme? Consider Margaret, one of the people profiled in *Habits of the Heart*, a sociological study on the growing individualism in the U.S. "I tend to operate on the assumption that what I want to do and what I feel like is what I should do."[6] Or read Laura Beth Jones in *Jesus CEO*: "I shape my own destiny. What I believe, I become. What I become, I can do."[7] Again, it is all about me. The *I's* still have it.

Even trends in worship patterns in the U.S. church reflect this narcissistic, self-focused change. Look at the lyrics for the older, more traditional hymns that dominated Christian church music for centuries. Compare those lyrics to today's genre of praise and worship music that has swept the Christian worship scene, creating intergenerational chaos in its wake. The most notable change is the dramatic increase in the use of the words *I* and *me*. While many would note a dramatic increase in the average Christian's depth of personal response in worship, it has not come without a price tag. That cost may include diminished unity and community in churches and the Church at large! If it's all about me, it's hard for it to be about us in a community called and designed by God to be interdependent.

*Entitlement*, the second word used in the kids' marketing article, adds an intriguing dimension to our look at individualism: "Not only is it about me, and I want what I want because I want it, but I want what I want because I *deserve* it." Entitlement encourages an attitude of personal advantage. By self-proclaimed merit, one deserves what one has, wants, or needs. Period.

Does this attitude affect the church? In my work with hundreds of churches, I have repeatedly heard comments reflecting a sense of *entitlement*. Here are some representative comments made by people as they depart one church for another:

> "Pastor, we have loved being a part of this church, but we feel led to leave at this time. Frankly, we believe we deserve better worship."

> "Joe, it's been a joy to be a part of this church plant over the past five years. Unfortunately, we are heading for another fellowship because, well, honestly, we feel like our kids deserve a better youth group."

*Deserve?* If Christians got what they deserved, it would not be a better church or worship experience or youth group — it would be hell! Christian's attitudes have changed, and an entitlement mentality is truly changing the present complexion of both the church at large and the local congregations.

> **If Christians got what they deserved, it would not be a better church or worship experience or youth group — it would be hell!**

The third piece of the marketing strategy to kids was to create *dissatisfaction*. From a marketing standpoint, if I want people to buy my products, I must first make certain that they are not happy or satisfied with what they already have, and encourage the want for more or different. Marketing strategies intend to create dissatisfaction with what is and with what I have — even with who I am. Consider the potential results of such a strategy:

> I am not happy with my job. ... I want a different job.

> I am not happy with my car. ... I want a new one.

I am not happy with my son's teachers. ... I should demand a new class or change schools.

I am unhappy about the way I look. ... I should use new cosmetics or get a face-lift.

I am really frustrated with my pastor, my small group leader. ... I should work to get rid of them or change churches.

I am dissatisfied with my marriage, with our kids. ... Hmm.

In this mode of unhappiness, when will I be content, the opposite of dissatisfied? When I get a new workout outfit or the SUV I have been coveting? How about transferring from church A to church B, to church C? Where does it end? In the eyes of the marketers, never!

Whatever happened to the call to contentment, modeled in Philippians 4:4-19? In a world where Jesus is Lord, and where he desires that we find contentment in him and him alone, how do we function in a cultural paradigm that expects us to eventually become dissatisfied with everything and everybody? Maybe individualism is a much deeper problem than many of us have considered.

This recent book on the subject was an eye-opener: *Affluenza: The All-Consuming Epidemic.*[8] How far can we go with over-consumption and over-work? Another recent book, *Becoming the Parent you Want to Be*, has an innocent sounding title. However, it essentially advocates over-playing to a child's needs for self-esteem and underplaying the desperate need for parental discipline.[9] Even the little *I*'s have it!

**From Russia Without Love.** This subject of individualism and its grandiose self-fulfillment became profoundly personal in Moscow, Russia, in 1995. I was a part of the CoMission movement, a five-year training process to prepare Russian schoolteachers to teach Christian moral ethics in their public schools.[10] Since this country had but one intact cultural structure after the fall of Communism — the schools — we believed God had given us a wide-open door to reach the whole former Soviet bloc with the Gospel. Our strategy as a CoMission group of 70 Christian mission groups working in concert was to function in 200 teams that worked in 65 different cities throughout the former Soviet Union. Through the process we were privileged to see many Russians, Ukrainians, Estonians, and others come to faith in Christ, leading to hundreds of new churches now glorifying God in the former heartland of Communism!

The life-altering moment for me, though, came three years into our five-year strategy. One of the Russians, who had accepted Christ and grown dramatically as a disciple, became a new team member on one of our teams. One day he came to an American teammate and offered this counsel: "I am so thankful that you American Christians brought Jesus Christ to our culture. But I have a suggestion. Would you please go home until your team members like each

> **Would you please go home until your team members like each other, and then come back and share the gospel?**

other, and then come back and share the gospel?"

When I heard this, I wept. Could it be that our American Christian culture had become so individualistic and unhappy that our teams did not even look or act like teams? Unfortunately, yes. Since that time, I have had many conversations, — not only with Russians but also with Kazakhs, Ukrainians, Tamil-speaking Indians, Shona tribal members in Zimbabwe, Malaysians, and others. They have confirmed what we learned that day in 1995: American evangelical Christians look and act very much like their narcissistic, entitled and unhappy culture, and have a difficult time working as part of a team.

Coming to grips with this truth was a painful learning process. Since CoMission was 98 percent Anglo-American, I used a culturally specific team-building illustration during a training session with our team leaders. My intent was to clarify the cost of working together. It was about a Canadian team and an American team climbing K2, the second highest mountain in the world. An American team member was complaining to a member of the Canadian climbing team camped several hundred meters away. The

> **American evangelical Christians look and act very much like their narcissistic, entitled and unhappy culture, and have a difficult time working as part of a team.**

American said. "I am tired of people on our team breaking into cliques and just doing their individualistic thing. Three or four of us [i.e., *my clique!*] will not put up with this any longer, so we are leaving the team." The Canadian looked at the American and said, "I don't know how you individualistic Americans ever get up a mountain together!"

Something very unexpected happened that became more important than my original purpose in telling this story. Every non-American in the room, five or six people from Commonwealth countries (Great Britain, Australia, New Zealand, and Canada) approached me personally at different times over the next 24 hours. Each one said essentially the same thing: "You have no idea how true this is about our American counterparts." What amazed me was that these were not Russians or Asians. They were from other English-speaking countries! And it happened with more Commonwealth folk over the next several training events. From this point on I realized that addressing the issue of American evangelical individualism would be a major part of my team-building work yet to come.

In the context of CoMission, the American leadership saw this five-year program as a materials-driven strategy. We had failed to understand that the Russian and Ukrainian cultures were relational. The majority of our CoMission trainers were more task or content-focused than relationally attuned in their training. We learned that content in books had to be embodied in real people — truth would be understood as trust developed in deeper relationships. In fact, I now have worked extensively in eight cultures, all in the non-Western world except for Mexico and the United States. Seven of the eight are relational cultures, where the primary currency for doing business in the culture is relationship. The U.S. culture is the *only* individualistic, materially dominated one.

The Frenchman Alexis de Tocqueville first identified the American propensity toward individualism — in the mid 1800's. "Tocqueville singled out family life, our religious traditions, and our participation in local politics as helping to create the kind of person who could...ultimately support free institutions.... He also warned that some aspects of our character — what he was one of the first to call 'individualism' — might eventually isolate Americans one from another and thereby undermine the conditions of freedom."[11] He was right.

I have one further concern about the impact of American individualism: we are exporting this model worldwide! As I travel throughout Russia, Central Asia, India, and Southeast Asia, among other places, I see individualism growing in the younger generation. In fact, everywhere that American marketing strategy — the model based on narcissism, entitlement, and dissatisfaction — is being utilized, I see the destructive side effects of an overt focus on the *I* over the *we*. Not only are we living out an individualistic lifestyle that has deeply invaded evangelical Christian culture, we are now infecting previously relational cultures around the world.

## Community: The Biblical Reality

We trainers in the CoMission movement were changed forever because of what happened in those five years from 1993-1998. For many of us, the CoMission model was God's tender hand working to transform our little band of Christian trainers from individualism to community, the biblical alternative. I now call it "moving from I to we," language we will develop more fully in chapter 7.

CoMission was a five-year course of action, and, with seventy Christian mission groups involved, we did not have the luxury of time to fine-tune strategy in great detail. Each group had to pitch in together and just trust God to give us direction on how to build the ship as we were sailing it. In the process, we learned to trust each other across different organizations as we shared the work and our lives at a profoundly personal level.

The result? We experienced the power of God as we shared training roles, with impact corporately that was far beyond what any of us could have done individually. And we saw that same power work across organizations to create unity that was beyond description. God worked powerfully among us on the training team through the five-year process to help us overcome our American individualistic tendencies. God broke down individual barriers, and his Spirit breathed a common life of synergy that none us had believed possible from our past experiences in our mission agencies.[12]

As a result of the CoMission years, I began to take a new look at a subject that had long been a priority in my discipling, mentoring, and training. The subject was community — the reality that it truly is all about relationships. I began to see some things in a new light.

John 17:20-26 suddenly took on a new depth of meaning. Why had Jesus, in his last personal time in the upper room with the disciples before he would go to the cross, focus on the importance of being one with his followers, even as he and the Father were one? Why had he prayed for us even as he prayed for those with him there in the flesh? And why had he interwoven the idea of the world believing the Father had sent the Son with this issue of unity in relationships?

> My prayer is not for them alone. I pray also for those who will believe in me through their message, that all of them may be one, Father, just as you are in me and I am in you. May they also be in us so that the world will believe that you have sent me. I have given them the glory that you gave me, that they

> may be one as we are one: I in them and you in me. May they be brought to complete unity to let the world know that you sent me and have loved them even as you have loved me.[13]

I have concluded that Jesus knew what we would be facing in the 21st century. He prayed for us future believers because he wanted to reveal to us, with all the saints since the resurrection, that life is still all about relationships. It began with the Father and the Son and flowed out into all Christians through the Holy Spirit, — that is, the "communion of the Holy Spirit." In the Trinity we have the original model of unity in relationship, so it has existed since before humankind was created. The Trinity was the original community! When the world turns to grand strategies and brilliant entrepreneurial creativity, God still desires that we remember the centrality of relationships, his ultimate strategy. Yes, God's global strategy is relational! When individualism and entitlement run roughshod over the traditional priorities of family and communities, the certainty of oneness remains. When people find ultimate dissatisfaction as they seek happiness in material things or political power or education or position, the primacy of relationships still stands at the heart of life for Christians and the whole body of Christ.

> **When the world turns to grand strategies and brilliant entrepreneurial creativity, God still desires that we remember the centrality of relationships, his ultimate strategy.**

Out of my CoMission experience, I also began to understand why both Paul and Peter discussed the primacy of people living in right relationship with each other from so many different relational angles: husband/wife, parent/child, employer/employee, believer/unbeliever. I had often wondered why Paul and Peter did not spend more time focusing on the tactics of evangelism, offering more intentional "how to's" for reaching the world for Christ. Suddenly I realized that both had done just that. Relationships such as living in unity at home as husband and wife, and having friendships with non-Christians in your world, realistically portray the community love of Christ for those searching for the meaning of life. It is all about relationships.

These so-called *oikos* relationships (Greek for "household or network of relationships") give us a major clue biblically into the importance of community in a world where form is often favored over substance, and where position is often valued over relationship. It is all about relationships, as John 17 showed us, oneness in relationship as the ultimate frame of reference revealing God the Father and his son Jesus to the world.[14]

Several years ago, there was a powerful video segment on a television news magazine about Zubaida, a young Afghan who had been badly burned and facially disfigured during the war in Afghanistan in the nineties. She was brought to America, where a plastic surgeon restored her physical appearance to near normalcy. During this long process of surgeries over several years, the plastic surgeon and his wife invited Zubaida to live with them. She consented, became part of their family, and began to live a normal upper-middle-class lifestyle in America. As Zubaida healed physically, she was given the choice to move back to live with her poor extended family in Afghanistan or continue living with her informally adoptive family and their comfortable Southern California lifestyle. The decision was easy for Zubaida. Though she would greatly miss the doctor and his wife, she would return home to her family. The shocked reporter asked, "How can she go back to life in Afghanistan after having everything that America has to offer?"[15]

The power of love revealed in family and community outweighs the value of the greatest palace. I remember visiting the Taj Mahal in Agra, India, praised as one of the world's most beautiful structures. Its exterior beauty can be understood more deeply when one realizes that Emperor Shah Jahan had it built in loving memory of his wife, Mumetz Mahal, in the 1600's. The physical structure is impressive, but the relationship is the source of the beauty of this structure that took 23 years of ornate crafting to build.[16]

Relationships in any culture are crucial. I have come to see serious weaknesses in the virtual team concept, and major strengths in face-to-face teams. God's design really does give priority to substance and process over form. His intent is for relationships to have priority over position or results. The call and strategy for world evangelization are still vital — that is certain. But how we fulfill the Great Commission is at issue. Consider that our common Western approach to evangelism over the past 30 years has been one-to-one sharing for individual conversions. Yet, several friends, long-term workers doing ministry in Central Asia, portray a serious problem with such an approach. In community-based cultures, they note, this style of individualistic conversions is hampering the ability to see the Gospel go down natural, family lines. In Acts 10, Cornelius and his family come to faith together, and such is a common model in India. Working with relationships among groups, not just with individuals, actually can dramatically change how you carry out your ministry strategy!

In fact, it is in the working out of the vision that God so often shows up in the process of the relationships. There he changes each one of us. Mountaineer Doug Scott sheds light on the nature of real community through his unique perspective on Himalayan mountain climbing as a team:

> [While climbing,] a lot of problems will arise between members. Climbing is no different from the classroom, the office, the factory floor; there will always be some degree of backbiting or argument — somebody feels that they are not getting recognition for what they are doing. The only difference is that when you are climbing, you can't walk away from it. You can't go home and forget it. You can't go down to the pub and drown your sorrows. You've got it twenty-four hours a day, so you do have to sort things out. Climbing does give you a chance to come to terms with yourself. What you find out about yourself is a gift.
>
> Everyone comes back changed from a long expedition to the high mountains. You're never quite the same person you were before.[17]

**The Role of Weakness in Creating Community.** As I have worked with hundreds of teams over the past fifteen years, I have spent a great deal of time thinking about the practical impact of American individualism. Interestingly, it is common for people from other cultures to say how much they value our rugged individualism because of how it brings out our pioneer spirit, that which frees us to risk trying new things. But even with that affirmation, what are the major factors that stand in the face of community?

We have already mentioned the most obvious: it is hard to live "we" when culture thinks and lives "I." Another way that this individualism plays out consistently is in what I call the "best foot forward" syndrome. When I meet people as an individual, I am very intentional about what I show people of myself. Wanting to look good, I show people my "best foot," that is, I show them the good qualities about myself. Why? I want people to like me and think well of me, so I seek to project that which is strong and positive about who I am and what I do. Seldom, if ever, will I show a weakness on purpose. That might cause you to think ill of me or to question my value to our group of friends or our team.

My favorite illustration in team-building seminars about the best-foot-forward syndrome is to offer this sample greeting: "Hello, it is nice to meet you. My name is Paul Ford, and I struggle with lust." Now, in our culture — or most cultures, for that matter — you just do not do such a thing! Why? It is culturally inappropriate. A person does not reveal weakness or liability in such a manner in the early stages of a relationship, if at all. In fact, that commonly is the problem: we never get to admitting weaknesses that each of us bring to the team. And it is those weaknesses, not the projected strengths, which commonly create the problems that divide teams members from one another.

I have found that the freedom to admit weaknesses and need to one another on a level playing field is one of the most important qualities of team life — and of real Christian community. We have known that admitting our sin and weakness to God is core to our respective personal relationships with God. But it is also a core part of healthy team life, essential for learning to value one another. In fact, through these team-building seminars I have discovered an amazing principle of life in the body of Christ.

> **God has also designed each one of us with intrinsic weakness — so that we would need others.**

God has designed each of us with great strengths to offer to one another. But God has also designed each one of us with intrinsic weakness — not sin, but rather areas where we are not as strong as others — so that we would need others. That is why together as the body of Christ we have such powerful impact. We literally become the living body of Jesus in the world, knowingly using our strengths but also openly admitting our weak areas, so that others in the body can fill those needy holes with their strengths. In Ephesians, Paul describes this amazing community concept: "From [Christ] the whole body, joined and held together by every supporting ligament, grows and builds itself up in love, as each part does its work."[18]

So then, when does real community happen? Does it occur when I show you my "good stuff," those attributes with which I can impress you? Or, does real community happen when each of us has a safe environment in which we can reveal our weaknesses and admit who and what we need from others? Clearly it is the latter. Once people find acceptance for who they are — both strengths and weaknesses — the first step toward deeper unity has been taken. Grace becomes a part of community life at this point in a very personal and corporate way.

Two assessment tools developed over the last ten years, the "Team Style Questionnaire" and the "Primary Functions of Leadership,"[19] are critical parts of my teambuilding strategy. Because of the tremendous impact of individualism on team life, I designed assessments that would give people a safe way to admit their weaknesses and their need for one another. People need a level playing field to move past their desire to impress one another and acknowledge their strengths and weaknesses and what kinds of people they need to round out who they are. Both assessments have language that helps people do this very thing. Consider this set of questions used to help build community through the open sharing of weaknesses:

1) Where are you powerful?

2) Where are you weak? (not sin areas, but natural weaknesses where you are simply not strong, by God's design)

3) Whom do you need?

Compare the above questions with the set of questions I have found to be more common in American culture and even in our evangelical subculture:

1) Where are you strong?

2) Where are you weak?

3) To what seminar can you go to strengthen your weakness?

The focus on the first set of questions is on the community. The focus in the latter set is on the individual. And the difference between the two is a major issue in present-day Christian community.

What is the strategic difference between individualism and community? Individualism encourages the sharing of strengths to portray my individual strengths and personal impressiveness, and confirms the fact that "I really do not need others." If I am weak, I get trained to eliminate my weaknesses, reaffirming that I can do things on my own. Community encourages the sharing of strengths and open acknowledgement of weaknesses, with the understanding that God has designed us to need one another and function interdependently. Stated simply, "I need you, and part of the way you will know that is by my choosing to admit my weaknesses and my need for others in the body of Christ."

**The Korean Connection.** I have recently had the privilege of working with Korean Christian leaders in many locations throughout the world. I remember doing a one-day seminar with a group of Korean pastors in Southern California several years ago. Toward the end of the day, I felt led to share about this very issue of God allowing weakness in each one of us so that, for body life reasons, we would intrinsically need others to make us all stronger as a team. As I shared, it at a time of day when sitting too long and tiredness have worn down participants' attention spans, a rustling started throughout the room. I noted this at the moment, but in my own tiredness did not give it another thought.

In a few minutes, we had our summary discussion about the day's interaction. I gave every person in the room the chance to share one sentence about what was of practical, take-home value. I was overwhelmed that fifteen or sixteen in the group of twenty-five made specific reference to this issue of God designing personal weakness in each one of us (some stated, "God allows us to have weakness") so that everyone in the body of Christ can play their significant parts. Never before had I seen such a focus on one principle in the hundreds of seminars I have done, nor have I seen it since.

After this seminar I discovered what had happened. The event host, also a Korean, came running to me. Shockingly, he put a hand on each shoulder and shook me. Koreans generally are among the most polite people that I know, so I guessed something was up before he spoke! He said, "You don't know what you did!"

I responded, "Excuse me?"

He continued, "You set them free, Paul. Korean pastors are not allowed to have weaknesses. They are supposed to be all things to all people — meeting every need, up at 5 a.m. for every prayer meeting, doing all the ministry. If they do not honor their people with how hard they work and meet needs, they are shamed and dishonored. You confirmed that God allows for weakness in us — even has designed it into our make-up. This is unbelievable!"[20]

It took me several more years to fully comprehend what happened that day. What I actually discovered, by complete accident, was the lynchpin to (1) releasing Korean pastors from the guilt and control of authoritarian-style leadership by affirming weakness as a part of God's design and (2) validating why it is essential for them to openly share leadership functions with others, opening up team ministry possibilities so that body life can happen with greater power and impact, and enable deeper fellowship.

# Conclusion

It is not about me;  It's about us. It is not about what I can do as a leader in the power of God, but rather about how I can be a steward of my part and help others be stewards of their parts in body life. The move from *I* to *we* has begun!

Finally, it is truly amazing to realize that, in God's wisdom through the ages, his timing in this call to community fits perfectly with the postmodern world in which we now live. At the beginning of this chapter I referenced several concerns about postmodern values and community. As we close, consider three strategic realities going on in that same 21st century postmodern world, as Reggie McNeal outlines in *The Present Future*. Even in the heart of individualism, the reality of our connectedness is revealed, and the search for authentic spiritual meaning continues in community.

> This last notion introduces the other major tenet of postmodern thought - that we are all connected, that no one is isolated. The digital revolution and computers have made individuals both independently powerful and amazingly connected at the same time.[21]

> The science of quantum physics also contributes to this new way of thinking . The quantum universe is not a universe of things but a universe of relationships. ... The quantum vision of the universe is more interested in the whole, in how things interrelate. ... The quantum universe is a created universe, a giant thought, not a giant thing of modernism. It evidences design and intentionality, not randomness and natural selection. Room for God is growing in the postmodern world.[22]

> Postmoderns are wildly spiritual. It is a spiritualism that reflects a hunger for meaning and connectedness. ... Redemption in postmodernism is about loving others and serving others (Hard Rock Cafe: love all, serve all).[23]

It is in such a postmodern world that God calls us from individualism to community! Since he is the one who designed individuals with individual uniqueness, that same God has made a world that screams for me to find my connectedness — first to him and then to others seeking him. Christian community, the body of Christ, is the place to find my wholeness and my place, the final result of my search for meaning and sharing relationships. Let us be a part of this new wineskin of grace that, in Christ, frees individuals to discover their corporate place that God has prepared for them since time began!

## Endnotes for Chapter 2

[1]  Wechsler, Pat. "Hey Kid, Buy This!" (*Business Week*, June 30, 1997), p 64.

[2]  Ibid, p 63.

[3]  Reber, Arthur S., and Reber, Emily S. *Dictionary of Psychology* (London: Penguin Books, 2001), p 225.

[4]  Chessher, Melissa. "I Demand Satisfaction," (*American Way*, May 1, 2003), p 58.

[5]  Ibid., p 57.

[6]  Bellah, Robert N., and Madsen, Richard et al. *Habits of the Heart*, (NY, San Francisco: Harper & Row, 1985), p 14.

[7]  Jones, Laura Beth. *Jesus CEO* (New York: Hyperion Books, 1995), p 295.

[8]  de Graaf, John, Wann, David, and Naylor, Thomas H. *Affluenza: The All-Consuming Epidemic* (Berrett-Koehler, 2001).

[9]  Tsing Loh, Sandra. "The Marshall Plan" (*The Atlantic Monthly*, March 2005), pp 115-116.

[10]  Johnson, Paul, et al. The CoMission (Chicago: Moody Press, 2004)

[11]  Bellah and Madsen, *Habits of the Heart*, p vii.

[12]  Johnson, *The CoMission*

[13]  John 17:20-23.

[14]  New Testament passages in Ephesians, Colossians and 1 Peter will be discussed in detail in Chapters 4, and 5.

[15]  "Zubaida" (New Hudson, MI: ABC News Productions, 2003), video.

[16]  *www.encyclopedia.laborlawtalk.com/Taj_Mahal.*

[17]  O'Connor, Nicholas, ed. *Beyond Risk* (Seattle, WA: The Mountaineers), p 156.

[18]  Ephesians 4:16.

[19]  Both of these assessments can be found in Dr. Ford's two workbooks, *Discovering Your Ministry Identity* and *Your Leadership Grip* (St. Charles, IL: ChurchSmart Resources, 1997 & 2001).

[20]  Quote from a Korean partner in ministry, Kong Choon Taek.

[21] McNeal, Reggie. *The Present Future* (San Francisco: Jossey-Bass/Wiley, 2003), p 57.

[22] Ibid.

[23] Ibid.

# CHAPTER THREE

## Build Me Up and Put You Down

We were meant to live for so much more.
Have we lost ourselves?
> Switchfoot, contemporary Christian rock group

The wealth of the rich is their fortified city;
They imagine it an unscalable wall.
> Proverbs 18:11

I have seen more pastors destroyed by the false illusion
created by the idea that "anyone can be a leader and build a
big church" than any other thing.
> Bert Waggoner, U.S. Director Association of
> Vineyard Churches

An overseas American missionary and I were immersed in conversation. He had heard my introductory team-building message on cultural issues that tear apart unity in ministry teams. He heard my concern about how Americans are noted for their wanting everything in their lives to be bigger, better, higher, smarter, more powerful, more beautiful, or more popular. We began to dialogue about the stewardship of who he is and where God is calling him to be in the next season of his ministry. For a number of reasons, he was hoping for a certain position.

And then came the truly chilling words that still resound in my ears: "It's all about raising myself up in our organization." I was dumbstruck. It seemed as though he missed approximately 85 percent of my words in the previous hour!

"If the American dream is based on anything, it is on the idea that anybody can make it to the top."[1] That British perspective from *The Economist* magazine strikes a strong chord in the heart of America. "Keeping up with the Joneses'" is what we used to call it. But the more-and-better attitude has taken on a whole new level of cultural influence after twenty-five years of unprecedented increase in material wealth. "The wealth of the rich is their fortified city; they imagine it an unscalable wall."[2] However this attitude now affects much more than money or material success. It also includes professional success and increase or growth in almost any area of our lives. And, as with narcissism, entitlement, and dissatisfaction — the major attitudes in our individualism — it has become very difficult to tell the Christian from the non-Christian.

What makes me so confident that there is a ladder to climb for those in full-time Christian ministry? Over the past fifteen years, I have had hundreds of conversations with pastors, missionaries, and Christian leaders in seventy denominations and numerous theological backgrounds. Seldom have I found people who are content where they are and in what they are doing. Like our Marketing 101 discussion in the last chapter, far and away the majority seem unable to find joy in being who they are, or where they are, at present. For some reason, most believed that there was something ahead that would be more exciting, or would finally be the place for which they had been searching. The most intriguing thing, though, is that the desire to move into another position is always tied to a perceived "upward" movement, or a lateral movement to a position more strategic for a future move to a perceived "higher" role. Why?

Well, bigger is better, higher is better — of course. If we put together myth number one, that everyone can and should be a leader (closer to the top or nearer to the front) and myth number two, that it's all about me, the natural result is that I should seek to climb to the highest perch available. Add Marketing 101, which also encourages dissatisfaction about where I am or how I look — even who I am — why would I not push ahead or higher or for more or better? The ladder mentality gives me the opportunity to climb to my heart's content.

When I was ten years old, my father, a pastor, was considering a move to a church in another state. What piqued my interest — even at that young age — was that Dad was prayerfully considering the possibility of moving to a church smaller than his present church. I asked my father, "Dad, why would you go to a church that is smaller than this one?" I already understood the ladder-climbing mentality at age ten, with no special training. Move up, lead more people, because bigger is better. Christians simply translate it into spiritual terms. It is still about "building me up." (I am saving my father's response for later in this chapter.)

Somehow I forgot the lesson I learned that day. In my early twenties, I was confident that there indeed was a ladder to climb in ministry. I was a youth ministry intern in northern North Dakota, and was having coffee with a man in our church. Wanting to affirm me, he said, "Paul, you are doing such a great job with our youth that, someday, I believe you could actually pastor your own church!" His intended message was one of affirmation for the quality of work I was doing. But what I heard tells a great deal about what was already true in my perception of professional Christian ministry arena. I heard, "Paul, someday you can climb higher on the Christian ladder if you play your cards right!"

## Our Search for Significance.

As I met with more and more Christian leaders searching to "move up" or somehow become, in their eyes, "more important in the kingdom," I pondered this attitude long and hard, especially as I was doing team-building seminars with Christian leadership teams across the denominational and mission theological spectrum. When people are climbing, this has a dramatic impact on how they work together in a given ministry. If in real estate it is all about "location, location, location," in Christian cultures where the ladder mentality is being played out, it is all about "position, position, position." In the context of team dynamics, even Christians get protective, possessive, or envious of others in "higher" positions.

Even the twelve apostles grasped this concept and became the first kingdom climbers: "They came to Capernaum. When he was in the house, he asked them, 'What were you arguing about on the road?' But they kept quiet because on the way they had argued about who was the greatest."[3] Shortly after this event, at the next stop in the region, James and John tried a new angle to position themselves as greatest in the kingdom alongside Jesus. "'Teacher,' they said, 'we want you to do whatever we ask.' Jesus responded, 'What do you want me to do for you?' They replied, 'Let one of us sit on your right hand and the other sit on your left in glory.'"[4]

There is a deeper issue underlying all of this ladder climbing. After ten years of coaching hundreds of Christian leaders in the stewardship of who they are, I now stand convinced: Beneath the climbing and pushing and grasping for more is the search for personal significance.

> **Beneath the climbing and pushing and grasping for more is the search for personal significance.**

Without God, the desire to prove one's sense of value through things or people or position or popularity is the norm. The brokenness and insecurity of humanity leads many people to the felt need of validating themselves before others. We can, step away from this pursuit by allowing God's grace in Christ to cover us and make us fully worthy and totally accepted in our significance.

Yet Christians still battle with significance issues. The cultural pressures described in chapter 2, as well as any ongoing battle with sin or relational hurt, can create serious internal conflict. In that unsettledness, we may be inclined to climb back on the ladder, searching for earthly confirmation of something that only God can give. With this renewed intent to climb for something better or more or higher, God's grace seems insufficient. It is blocked by the hurt or sin to which we hold. Thus we seek approval and validation on the ladder of significance, desiring to "move up" and again prove our worth. This search for significance leads many Christians to what I call the "Jesus plus" approach to securing our worth on a daily basis.

Let's take a brief personal inventory. What makes you significant? Upon what or in what or whom do you seek to find your worth or value? If you are a Christian, I am fairly confident that you would include God or Jesus as the source of your significance. But consider the possibility that there are one or two areas where you replace God's grace with your own attempts to prove your worth. Think about the following categories as potential areas where you might be on the ladder, out to prove yourself by moving up or attaining more. In addition to your relationship with God, do you find significance in any of the following:

- Beauty
- Education/degrees
- House
- Material possessions
- Money/financial worth

- Popularity

- Political influence

- Position at work or other places

- Power

- Relationships with people of significance

- Status

- Success

- Travel

Unlike George Leigh Mallory, the first man to die attempting to climb Mount Everest, we don't climb simply "because it is there." We have our reasons — our very personal, often deeply rooted reasons.[5] And so we climb. In the process, we as individuals miss out on life in the body of Christ and as teammates often thwart that which God intends to do among us in our church or ministry.

While this exhorter-prophet would prefer challenging you at this point, I want to share a part of my own search for significance as a Christian. In 1995, I had my first book, *Unleash Your Church!*, published along with several workbooks which accompanied that original leader's guide to mobilizing the body of Christ. Though I did not understand this at that time, I can now tell you that one of the underlying reasons I wrote that first book was to prove my worth and value as a Christian leader.

Somehow I had received and believed the message that if I could write a book that other Christian leaders would actually read, it would finally prove that I was worth something as a Christian leader. That is, I wanted to become a man of fame, of importance, to finally validate my worth as a leader. I did not want a lot of personal glory — just enough to heighten my place and position in the kingdom to where people would notice.

However, I had forgotten one important principle: God will not share his glory with anyone! Rather, he has made relationship to have priority over position. There is no ladder to climb in the kingdom, only relationships in which to be faithful. Near the point of my chance for increased self-importance, he took me to the "spiritual woodshed" to help me understand how he works relationally by removing any chance for wide recognition or positional glory. I quickly moved from an ascent

**There is no ladder to climb in the kingdom, only relationships in which to be faithful.**

that was nearing the top of the mountain to lying flat on my back in the desert.

Just as the major promotion for my book was beginning, a series of financial crises threatened the very existence of my publisher. In fact, within eighteen months, the business closed its doors. The first major plight was that I and other authors were owed royalty money. This shocking reality became a part of the brokenness through which God allowed my family to walk. To start our ministry, we had borrowed against the anticipated royalties of the first three to four years. Suddenly we had significant debt. We had to sell our first home to pay off that debt.

And I abruptly became my own publisher and distributor. My wife Julie and I began to sell my book and workbooks out of our garage for four years. But now God began to reveal his glory on his terms. The materials began to sell nationwide with no promotion. People just started calling and placing orders. God began to meet our financial need unrelated to anything that Sarah (my administrative assistant), Julie, or I did. Friends in ministry from around the U.S. and Canada obviously encouraged people to buy our materials. But the growth in material sales still made no sense — only God could have caused the increase in sales with no formal advertising anywhere in the U.S. In fact, during those first four years I tried three different marketing plans to sell the materials — but never broke even on one of them!

Through this desert time, God began to teach Julie and me to love him and him alone, and to trust his provision in every facet of our lives. God was also beginning to untie my need to prove my worth as a great leader by climbing the leadership ladder. I took my first major jump off the ladder and began to find God's grace to be sufficient. For God to gain my full attention, it took the financial loss of a home, a season of ill health for my wife, and the loss of my potential fame. Living a life for God has nothing to do with how I seek to position myself on the ladder, be it in life, ministry or leadership. This life-changing principle began to take root in our lives: life really is about the stewardship of relationships as God provides.

**The Issue of Authoritarian Leadership.** Another sobering confirmation of the pervasiveness of this ladder-climbing myth emerges from my multicultural work. I have worked actively in eight cultures on four continents over the past twelve years doing team-building with teams across each of these cultures. I have found only one problem consistently the same in every culture: authoritarian leadership. Every culture battles with the issue of leaders wanting to climb to the top and control people and things.

This should not be a surprise when we recall Satan's words as he was tempting Jesus in the desert: "Again, the devil took Him to a very high mountain and showed him all the kingdoms of the world and their splendor. 'All this I will give you if you will bow down and worship me.'" (Matthew 4: 8-9) To rise up like a king and rule over all! The opportunity to be surrounded by power and splendor is more than just a temptation. In every culture where I have ministered, I have found pastors and Christian leaders — even small group leaders — who want to take such authoritarian control.

This desire for power and control is unquestionably one of the most dramatic forms of the search for significance in cultures worldwide. And it is also one of the most common problems that breaks apart teams: the desire for control of people and their actions, even to the point of withholding leadership functions from others so that no one can question the importance of one's position or authority. What better way to prove that I can be my own lord, in full control of everything and everyone around me?

Alexander was a young pastor leading a Russian church of one hundred people, having inherited the group from another pastor who had left the country. With newfound freedom in Russia, people in the church were excited about the opportunities they would have to share in ministry through their cell groups, which had been the backbone of the church's growth. But Alexander, though inspirational and friendly in his style, was concerned by the great freedom given to the cell leaders in pastoring their groups. He feared that leaders would take their small groups and start new churches without his permission as the pastor.

So his first major action in his new role was to limit the freedom of the cell group leaders to lead their groups. No leader could invite a cell group member to any kind of service without first receiving permission from the pastor. And no group could initiate any informal outreach with only their own cell group involved. Sadly, these decisions created a tremendous loss of freedom and joy both in cell leaders and their groups. Within a year, the church fell to thirty-five members and, more strategically, lost six cell groups. Those who remained were either in the pastor's cell or were not involved in a group.

Koreans have a unique style of addressing this leadership dilemma.

One of their serious cultural concerns is that you cannot share leadership responsibilities because those with whom you share will take advantage of your leadership and put you down — even try to steal your position. Thus their approach to starting new ministries is very unusual. Everywhere I go in the world, I find that most Korean ministry teams are made up of only one couple! That is, the way many Koreans solve the problem of sharing leadership is for a single couple to start and maintain the ministry. That removes the competition for position and the need to share important leadership functions with others from the beginning of the new work.

The problem of authoritarian leadership existed in the church in the 1500's, the era of the Reformation. The reformers, battling the authority of the Roman Catholic Church and its leadership, sought to acknowledge the biblical principle of the priesthood of all believers. The body life model portrays every believer literally as one of the priests — a true representative of God among the people. Yet that cornerstone principle was never fully realized then — or since. Given that, should we be surprised that authoritarian leadership is the most common issue across multiple cultures to this day? It is time to move away from such patterns and the unhealthy search for significance through climbing the ladder, and recapture God's first-century wine so that we can find freedom from the need to be climbers.

## The Biblical Reality of Stewardship

God desires that we be his kingdom builders, committed to the task of stewardship of what he has prepared in our lives and those he entrusts to us. The desire for earthly kingdom climbing pervades our culture, but God has designed a different model through his grace.

Allow me to finish my story about Dad and his call to the smaller-sized church. When I asked him why he would go to a smaller church, he looked at me with a twinkle in his eyes. My father had a melancholy-type personality, so when I saw his eyes sparkling I knew I was going to get something special from him at that moment. He said, "Son, the only reason that I am going to a smaller church is because I believe that is where God wants me to be." We moved to that new church and new town, and I watched Dad and Mom faithfully serve, equip, and release those whom God gave them.

That moment with my father significantly changed my perspective. I did forget that lesson for a number of years during my early twenties — my "climbing" season. However, I now know that life is no longer about climbing to higher places or positioning myself for greater impact, but rather about learning to be a good steward of those whom God gives me in each season of life.

Let us consider ladder climbing for a moment. This may actually be our way of trying to help God position ourselves properly from our own perspective and needs. Bear this in mind as the Apostle Peter speaks vividly to us. It appears that God sees this issue a bit differently:

> All of you, clothe yourself with humility toward one another, because,
>
> "God opposes the proud but gives grace to the humble."
>
> Humble yourselves under God's mighty hand, that he may lift you up in due time.[6]

If there is any lifting up to be done, God will be the architect of that. He does not need our help! He does not need my attempts to position myself for upward movement or for favor in the eyes of others.

Leadership is a function of responsible service in the kingdom, not a position to be praised or glorified. First Thessalonians 5: 12-13 does encourage us to respect and honor those who are over us. But it does not place leaders in a higher position than others, to be perceived as more important or even more strategic. Leadership in action is actually a series of functions most powerfully fulfilled by a group of people. We will always have people who fill positions of leadership because God wants all of us to learn how to follow. But positional leadership is something designed by God and not by humans — for God to fulfill his intended purposes.

> **Leadership is a function of responsible service in the kingdom, not a position to be praised or glorified.**

With this introduction, then, what is our responsibility? What is the biblical model that replaces ladder climbing? In 1 Peter 4: 10-11, Peter challenges us to be good stewards of God's grace:

> *Each one should use whatever gift he [or she] has received to serve others,*
>
> *[as stewards] faithfully administering God's grace in its various forms.*
>
> *If anyone speaks, he should do it as one speaking the very words of God.*

*If anyone serves, he should do it with the strength God provides, so that in all things God may be praised through Jesus Christ.*

*To him be the glory for ever and ever. Amen.*

Here we see that the role of every Christian, including Christian leaders is to be a good steward. First, God calls us to use our individual gifts to serve others, with the "I" powerfully prepared to serve the "we." Why? Because we are called to be good stewards or superintendents; that is, we are called to be effective household managers of his multi-faceted grace. By his grace, God gave each of us powerful spiritual gifts that we are to wisely act as stewards for and employ for his purposes.

For biblical stewards, God has also prepared the right relationships, the people in whom we are to invest ourselves. Biblical stewards are Christians who learn to be who they are according to their spiritual gifts, but also manage their relationships with others whom God has brought into their lives. God has done all the preparation, and we manage what and with whom he has prepared! We are not kingdom climbers but kingdom builders, managing the grace gifts and the relationships he has given. We build what he gives, with whom he gives it.

Many people see Nehemiah as one of the best biblical models of leadership. They love to point out the way he surveyed the ruins of Jerusalem, and the way he prayed for God to restore the walls and his people, and the way he went to the king to gain favor for rebuilding the walls of Jerusalem. I am always surprised that Nehemiah 3 is seldom mentioned. This passage offers a vital illustration essential for understanding leadership today. Nehemiah lists which family is working on what part of the Jerusalem walls or gates. We do not know if Nehemiah the great leader ever touched a brick or a piece of wood. All we know is that he released all the people to play their parts in the rebuilding of Jerusalem!

> **The responsibility of the 21st century kingdom leader is to manage or coordinate whatever spiritual gifts — the power — that God gives, with whomever God gives — the people.**

In that chapter Nehemiah models this very principle of stewardship that we will discuss further in Section II. Nehemiah lists the *who* that God had prepared to build the walls and gates — His people, and he also listed the *what* — the powerful part each one was to play. The responsibility of the 21st century kingdom leader is to manage or coordinate whatever spiritual gifts — the power — that God gives, with whomever God gives — the people.

This stewardship principle has radically changed my life and my ministry. Come along and join me in this calling to be stewards of the body of Christ — its players and its gifts — as God has prepared for us. There is no need to climb any ladders. You are released. It is time to go deeper in understanding God's organic model.

## The Sarcasm Myth (Put You Down)

**The tongue has the power of life and death, and those who love it will eat its fruit.**
Proverbs 18:21

Before we look more intently at the organic body-life model, let us examine one last mythical piece to this leadership ladder puzzle. Some leaders build themselves up by tearing others down with the use of sarcasm — humor that is at someone else's personal expense. It is intended to make fun of a personality quirk or physical feature or what someone does or says. Someone pays the price when sarcasm is used. In what has become a cultural art form, sarcasm feeds the ladder mentality in the downward direction. It has become a highly valued form of humor in our culture. Sarcasm is based on the erroneous belief that everyone is (or should be) always able to take a joke — even one made up of harsh, spiteful words aimed at the heart of a person's weaknesses. While Americans do not have a corner on this market worldwide, we definitely are on the cutting edge.

The first talk I ever prepared, thirty years ago, related directly to the nature of sarcasm. The major premise was this: if I do not feel good about myself, about who I am or about how I am perceived by others, there are a number of things that I may do in response. The last item I shared was this: "If I do not feel good about myself, I will put others down to build myself up."

The ladder works both ways. Sometimes we pull ourselves up the ladder by pushing others down — or off — so that they will not be in the way of our climbing. While this may not seem like a nice thing to do, some people determine that it may be necessary to protect themselves from the threat others seem to represent with their gifts, vision, or heart.

Even with that early message about sarcasm, I had never thought it as a cultural problem until a trip to Moscow during my early travels into the former Soviet Union. During this trip, a Russian asked me this question: "What is it when Americans say mean things to each other and then laugh?" I laughed and said, "Why, that is sarcasm." Then suddenly I stopped laughing. We had already begun to grieve the reality that Russians were uncomfortable on our CoMission teams because of the individualism and entitlement attitudes they saw among us. Now a Russian was identifying sarcasm!

Then came a trip to Vladimir, Russia, in the late nineties, my fifth or sixth CoMission trip working with teams made up of mostly Americans and Russians. My translator for this event was Galya. After the session on cultural values in which I had made clear reference to this American use of sarcasm as a block to team body life, we took a break. I began to walk out of the room and happened to be right behind Galya. On the way out, she and I both overheard two Americans making sarcastic comments to each other and laughing uproariously. Then Galya, not realizing I was still within earshot, made this comment: "There go the Americans, being sarcastic with one another again." It was not only what she said, but also the sadness with which she said it, that caught me off guard. How clearly we can see and feel our cultural issues through the eyes of other cultures.

Russians have their own issues. Sarcasm just does not happen to be one of them. They are so blunt in general that sarcasm would have no real value as a form of communication. I realize now, though, it was that blunt honesty that helped me come to grips with the serious unity problem that sarcasm creates on teams of Americans wherever I go.

In my early years, I had never thought of sarcasm in negative terms. In fact, I am a recovering "sarcastaholic." I learned in my middle school years to use sarcasm to protect myself. During those years I was terribly overweight and was the brunt of many jokes from my peers. I finally determined that if you were going to insult me, you were going to pay a price. I had always been good with words, and so I began to fight back. Whenever anyone would be sarcastic or spiteful toward me, I would come back with a brilliantly (I thought) cutting remark, and that usually stopped the sarcasm short.

I became quite proficient at sarcasm and found that it was my quickest way to gain popularity in most settings. I found that I could build myself up by putting others down. I went up the ladder by pushing them down. It seemed to be an effective method for saving me a lot of grief and protecting my tender heart.

However, sarcasm interferes with community in a team setting. It creates an additional layer of protective cover against intimacy among team members. While most people will defend sarcasm as a way that "we endear ourselves to each other", I have found that not to be the case for all the people involved. It can be a form of bonding for two people with a long history who have established a high trust level. Not so for those who are watching two such friends and are new to the team. I know from years of working with teams that, without question, use of sarcasm builds calluses against team unity. People put on an extra layer of armor to protect themselves from getting hurt. In that way, intimacy is dramatically impaired, all in the name of "everyone can take a joke."

Perhaps we should not be surprised. One of the most dramatic examples of spiteful commentary in the public arena early in the new millennium was on the television show *The Weakest Link*. It was an early representative of the reality shows that now bombard Americans on a nightly basis. The putdowns and sarcasm offered by contestants toward one another was undoubtedly excessive, but that was the name of the game. Build yourself up at the expense of the weakest link! As a current commentator describes: "'Reality' shows now regularly feature a contestant addressing the camera, sharing his or her 'innermost thoughts' about, primarily, other players or contestants. Most reality TV programs seem to be little more than elaborate constructs to get their participants into these makeshift confessionals [of antagonism or plain old mean-spiritedness]. The result is a sort of psychological pornography."[7]

Consider briefly another vantage point on how the propensity toward putting others down is manifest within evangelical culture. In a *Christianity Today* article, Philip Yancey notes that one of the great things about evangelicals is that they will do anything, but he also makes these observations. "I love evangelicals. You can get them to do anything. The challenge is, you've got to soften their judgmental attitudes before they can be effective."[8] He also writes, "A journalist working in the New York media told me that editors have no qualms about assigning a Jewish person to a Jewish story, a Buddhist to a Buddhist story, or a Catholic to a Catholic story, but would never assign an evangelical to an evangelical story. 'Why not?' 'You can't trust them. They're judgmental'"[9] Sometimes our harshness is seen even by others to go beyond cultural norms.

After working with hundreds of American ministry and leadership teams, here are what I have learned to be the rules of sarcasm. On a team of ten people, there are commonly two or three world-class sarcas-taholics, and the others just play along. But everyone knows the rules. Everyone is supposed to take a joke. If someone is sarcastic with you, it is appropriate to respond immediately with another barb. Commonly, if you break the unwritten rules of the sarcasm game and say, "What you said was very hurtful for me," the game changes. The common response to such an expression of hurt is, "What is the matter? Can't you take a joke?!" And the game goes on.

I can tell you unequivocally that sarcasm does not build unity among leaders and teams! If you have a close friend with whom you can be sarcastic in endearing ways, do it privately and not in a team setting. Put a new rule in place on your team. If you are hurt by something another team member says to you, go to them and express the hurt. Break the rules of the sarcasm game.

This issue is not simply a leadership team or small group issue, but also something about which leaders in general must be careful. After one of our CoMission training sessions, a leader from one of the larger mission groups came to me with a personal concern. He said that their mission has established a disturbing pattern at major conferences: whoever introduces the speaker for the event sarcastically jokes about the speaker. The common response from the speaker, as you would expect, is to come back "returning the favor" and be equally sarcastic toward whoever did the introduction. Such modeling by primary leadership only reinforces the problem and reaffirms sarcasm as an honored value in the organization.

Another way I experienced the depth of this problem in Christian culture came while I was speaking at a conference in Colorado Springs five years ago. I was working with a group of mission executives. Up to that point in my ministry, I used to have a routine where I would make humorous references to my baldness. I would say such things as, "In this season of life, God has placed a special blessing on short, balding people," or "not only are the very hairs of my head numbered by God, but also the days of the very hairs of my head!" My goals were to show comfort with myself as I am and to show I could laugh at myself in talking about something in myself that others might see as a weakness.

However, those are not the messages that people received. They heard, "Paul Ford can make fun of himself, so I can make fun of him too!" And the sarcasm began to roll. At this particular conference, it got so bad that someone yelled something extremely sarcastic about my baldness from the very back of the auditorium, and the whole crowd roared with laughter. At that point, I realized that I had to stop modeling what people were reading as self-sarcasm. That is how embedded sarcasm is in our Christian culture in America. In forty overseas trips, never once has anyone publicly said a sarcastic word to me or any other speaker with whom I have worked. Different cultures have different issues. Here in America, we have a sarcasm problem.

## The Encouragement Reality

God calls us to build up, not to tear down, and not just individually, but in community: "And let us consider how we can spur one another on to love and good deeds. Let us not give up meeting together, as some are in the habit of doing, but let us encourage one another – and all the more as you see the Day approaching" (Hebrews 10: 24-25). This certainly applies to the kind of words you use in conversation.

Years ago, when my son Stephen was ten, he drew my attention to these words in Philippians, long after I had forgotten them in my sarcastaholic stupor: "Finally, brothers, whatever is true, whatever is noble, whatever is right, whatever is pure, whatever is lovely, whatever is admirable – if anything is excellent or praiseworthy – think about such things" (Philippians 4:8). If spiteful or hurtful thoughts escape from the mind and head for the mouth, "Do not let any unwholesome talk come out of your mouths, but only what is helpful for building others up according to their needs, that it may benefit those who listen" (Ephesians 4:29).

In the world of individualism, as I search out and secure the position that I "deserve" regardless of the cost to others, sarcasm is an accepted tool. Putting others down is just a part of the climbing game, even a sport or an art form in which the idea is to be the best at "slicing and dicing." But the Apostle Paul clearly reveals that we are to consider others before any words come out of our mouths. We must think first about the needs of others and whether or not what we say will be of help to them. Then we should consider how it will benefit – or not benefit – others who are within earshot. Paul continues, "Get rid of all bitterness, rage and anger, brawling and slander, along with every form of malice. Be kind and compassionate to one another, forgiving each other, just as in Christ God forgave you"(Ephesians 4: 31-32).

For years, I have used a special activity called an affirmation bombardment, where people each receive brief, specific affirmations from others in their group or team. My primary purpose is to stand up to a world of sarcasm and negativism with words that build up, not tear down. I have yet to find a team anywhere in the U.S. where words of affirmation are used more than sarcastic wit. On any given team within the first fifteen minutes of people introducing themselves, I find that anywhere from five to ten sarcastic witticisms are shared. This is true everywhere I go in the U.S., no matter what the mission culture or church theology; all groups tear down long before building up.

I long for affirmation — words that build up — to be a distinctive, new-millennium way that people will know who the Christians are. I will never forget the first time I used the affirmation bombardment exercise. I was a youth pastor in North Dakota. A group of middle school kids and I were gathered at a retreat center on the Canadian border.

> **Encouraging words that build up cut gently to the heart and often bring unity amidst disharmony or provide soothing balm amidst personal brokenness.**

If you not aware of the quantity and intensity level of sarcasm used in this age group, you are very fortunate. Why I started using the affirmation bombardment first with this age group, I will never know. It certainly was God who led us to that special event. Amazingly, the affirmation process took two hours, during which every youth shared and received vulnerably, and the majority of us wept for a portion of the two hours it took for us to go around the group. I knew this was a God thing when one of the boys asked if he could get some toilet tissue so that the girls and the boys would have something to dry the tears.

I knew from that day forward why building up is the name of the game for Christians. Encouraging words that build up, when offered in our sarcastic, individualistic, dissatisfied culture, cut gently to the heart and often bring unity amidst disharmony or provide soothing balm amidst personal brokenness.

I challenge you to consider your words and the contributions you make to building up and encouraging others on your team or in your ministry. Ask the Lord to soften your heart first, and then to put a guard over your mouth should this be a battleground issue for you. To this day, I have to watch my mouth. Sarcastic thoughts still squirm through my creative mind when someone says or does something that conjures up impulses of judgment, condescension, or sarcasm. I spent so many years quickly preparing the words that would cut like a knife that I need to have accountability in this area. I ask others to stop me the moment that I use any words that are sarcastic.

Thankfully, God has also given me a dear friend, Kemit, who has modeled a life of extreme encouragement. When Stephen was six years old, Kemit, a retired engineer, taught him to build balsa wood model airplanes. When I was not traveling, I got to share in the fun. On

Saturday mornings, there was a small group of retired engineers that met to fly their rubber-band powered planes. Stephen and I would fly our homemade contraptions and often chase down the airplanes of others.

Over the years, I have spent literally hundreds of hours talking with Kemit and watching him interact with others – on the airplane field and in many others places. He builds people up. He finds the good things in others, even when the rest of us want to bad-mouth or disparage them. He hopes for the best and believes the best. He is the one person in my life who reminds me of 1 Corinthians 13:7. He always protects, always trusts, always hopes, always perseveres. His patient kindness and lack of rudeness or self-seeking are qualities that have revealed God's heart of loving kindness toward so many. Kemit is one of my walking life lessons and someone I will cherish as long as I live.

## Conclusion

So then, did you get the mythical story line? It is all about becoming a leader! You can be a leader, and it is all about you. And, culturally speaking, here is how we will help you. You, the individual, have permission to pursue the following plan of action:

- Build me – It's all about me, because I deserve it and I am just not happy.

- Build me up – Let's go higher, bigger, more, as it is all about positioning!

- Put you Down – Others just cannot get in the way, or they will pay!

However, we are exposing these myths for what they are. And we are beginning to tear down the leadership ladder! God's call is not for us to be great leaders who climb and have full license to judgmentally or humorously put others down to secure our respective places in the sun. Rather, the biblical realities portray those in Christian leadership to be equippers who intend to be good stewards of all those whom God brings. They are to be encouragers who actively build up and not tear down, and who are clear on the fact that God has intricately designed the "I" for the sake of the "we." That is, the individually endowed believer has been prepared to build up the body of Christ by following leaders or building team unity as a ligament supporting the whole body.

That is why those of us who oversee others must be good stewards so that the fullness of God's grace can be revealed in his people, the living body of Christ. And because of this, let us consider the new wine and new wineskins that will give us a clearly defined picture of his design for leaders, teams, and the whole church.

## Endnotes for Chapter 3

[1] "The Missing Rung in the Ladder," (*The Economist*, July 16, 2005), p 53.

[2] Proverbs 18:11.

[3] Mark 9:33-34.

[4] Mark 10:35-37.

[5] For a deeper look into issues related to your personal significance, go to *The Ascent of a Leader* by Thrall, McNicol, & McElrath,,(New York: John Wiley & Sons/Jossey-Bass, 2001).

[6] 1 Peter 5: 5-6.

[7] Coffin, Andrew. "An ever weakening link: Have bitter soul-barings become televison's last new frontier?" (*World* magazine, June 2, 2001)

[8] Yancey, Philip. "A Quirky & Vibrant Mosaic" (*Christianity Today*, June 2005), p 37.

[9] Ibid, p 28.

# SECTION II

## Fresh Full-bodied Wine

In their discussion of world history in *The Lessons of History*, Will and Ariel Durant make the following point about the role of the Roman Catholic Church during the time of the Reformation in the sixteenth century: "More and more the hierarchy spent its energies promoting orthodoxy rather than morality."[1] The church's structure was dominating the way people lived in relationship to the church and state, and even in relationship with one another.

For our present-day consideration, what if we changed the word *orthodoxy* to *organization* and *morality* to *organism*? Consider this sentence: "More and more evangelical leadership spends its energies promoting leadership- or vision-driven organization rather than healthy, multiplying relationships."

In section 1, we began to counter the leadership ladder and its cultural partners with Biblical realities. In Section II, let's do some additional homework using more fine wine from the New Testament. Our intent is to bring a greater depth of perception to our leadership discussion. Let's set the context for defining the biblical leader through some important first-century biblical concepts. We continue now with more vigor, beginning the move toward the identification of new wineskins in Section III.

Chapter 4 looks at the primary environment in which leaders functioned during the first-century A.D. Chapter 5 identifies what "leadership language" was used and the initial implications of those terms. Finally, chapter 6 explores the models derived from both assessment of the environment and descriptive language used by Jesus, Paul, and Peter. God's economy of grace will reveal clear guidelines as we seek understanding of biblical leadership.

# CHAPTER FOUR

## The Body of Christ and Biblical Leadership

*I am the vine; you are the branches. If a man remains in me, and I in him, he will bear much fruit; apart from me you can do nothing.... If you remain in me and my words remain in you, ask whatever you wish and it will be given you. This is to my Father's glory, that you bear much fruit, showing yourselves to be my disciples.*

*My command is this: love each other as I have loved you. Greater love has no one than this, that he lay down his life for his friends.... I no longer call you servants, because a servant does not know his master's business. Instead I have called you friends, for everything I learned from my Father I have made known to you. You did not choose me, but I chose you and appointed you to go and bear fruit — fruit that will last.*
    John 15: 5, 7-8, 12-13, 15

*From him the whole body, joined and held together by every supporting ligament, grows and builds itself up in love, as each part does its work.*
    Ephesians 4:16

The leadership realities of today noted in section I have developed over the past fifty-plus years through the development of a free-market economy. "We have come to understand economics as 'the science of how people produce goods and services, how they distribute them among themselves, and how they use them.'"[2] This market-driven economy started in the West but also has had great influence and impact throughout Asia. Amazingly, U.S. economic approaches are now returning to the U.S. from countries like China, Singapore, and India through cheaper products, outsourcing of labor, and even relocation of whole businesses! What an intriguing economic turn of events. Other countries are learning from and modeling many patterns from the U.S. economy to the point of becoming serious competitors worldwide.

God has his own economy, his own framework for fulfilling his desired ends. The word for "economy" or "administration," *oikonomian* in the Greek, appears in the New Testament, as found in Ephesians 3:2: "Surely you have heard about the administration [economy] of God's grace that was given for me to you." This word "economy" fits the literal meaning of that Greek word. Interestingly, God's system or economy of administering his grace to the world does not give concern to leadership language, individualism, entitlement, or ladder climbing. In fact, his economy of grace looks more like a life-giving, growing organism than a highly structured organization with strategic plans and expected results. Rather, "God has a new plan to introduce the making up and regulating of his household."[3]

This life-giving, organic nature, seen as a growing vine and its branches in John 15, is found in more places than just his kingdom work or even the church. Consider the natural, organic development of seeds, another piece of God's economy. My friend Larry Sallee, who sends seed varieties to more than fifty nations, writes:

> Organic, natural seed, or "open pollinated" seed, is the old-fashioned type where you can save the seed from year to year. In order to save the seed after harvest, you need to collect from many individual plants and mix them together to maintain the diversity for next year. This selection process has produced crops that will make a harvest under good and difficult years, rich organic soils and poor ones. Disease rarely wipes out the whole field, as some members carry resistance to pass back to the community of all the seeds. Hybrid seeds - developed by scientists - carry a very narrow gene pool. These seeds are extremely uniform genetically to take advantage of

only the best soils. They also need chemical fertilization in the field yearly and must have near perfect growing conditions to produce a crop. Hybrids do produce a larger harvest but the dollar investment is much larger than with organic crops.

The choice of which to use comes down to cost. Can you afford new seed every year, plus fertilizer, weed spray, and government crop insurance for that likely-to-show-up difficult year? Or do you trust the genetic diversity of organic seed to get you a crop, plus provide seed for the next year and the next? Remember: it is this less-expensive, natural seed that is able to get you through good and bad years, in excellent or poor soil.

It is the organic seed that I send to countries all over the world, not only because people in these places cannot afford the costs of seed genetically altered by man, but because it will make it through over the long haul — even in poor soil. I think God knew what he was doing with organic seed. He knows that multiplication of crops depends upon the healthy interaction of all the seeds in the community! [4]

And so we begin our look at the language and nature of God's economy, commencing our search that will lead us eventually to the concept of leadership and how it was understood and applied in the New Testament world.

> **He knows that multiplication of crops depends upon the healthy interaction of all the seeds in the community!**

## The Language of God's Economy: Community and Fellowship

Many people today believe that the local church is simply an organization like many other associations or groups of people. If the church were merely another human enterprise, it would make sense that we could freely adapt and apply secular leadership and management principles in the church.

But this organization came into being through the life, death, and resurrection of Jesus Christ! In Acts 1:8, just before his ascension into Heaven, Jesus told his followers that they would soon receive power when the Holy Spirit came upon them. Following that powerful move of the Spirit in Acts 2, his disciples multiplied in number and came to be called Christians. Those Christians formed into groups in hundreds of locations, and eventually came to be called the church in its various local settings.

What were key words used to describe this growing, vibrant fellowship of Christians? *Ekklesia* is the Greek word for church, the actual assembly or meeting together of Christians. Acts 5:11 is the first usage of this word. These groups meeting in those first few days through the first several centuries are very different than most organized churches and their buildings of today. The *ekklesia* was a small open fellowship of Christian disciples gathered for worship, usually in homes. Each gathering was understood not as a separate entity on its own, but rather as a local expression of the whole church of Jesus Christ.

> **"This means that the whole power of Christ is available to every local congregation, that each congregation functions in its community like the whole church functions in the whole world.**

What are the implications of this? "This means that the whole power of Christ is available to every local congregation, that each congregation functions in its community like the whole church functions in the whole world."[5] From the Day of Pentecost there grew a fellowship of people who saw their gatherings as the new temple, the place where God lived by his Spirit[6]. It was no longer housed in a building like the Jewish synagogue, but rather it was gatherings of the people of God in multiple local settings, where his Spirit lived and moved and had his way among them.

What did this mean for the Christians assembled together? After the powerful activity on the Day of Pentecost in Acts 2, our best picture of the initial activity of the earliest *ekklesia* comes from Acts 2:42-47:

> *They devoted themselves to the apostles' teaching and to the fellowship, to the breaking of bread and to prayer. Everyone was filled with awe, and many wonders and miraculous signs were done by the apostles. All the believers were together and had everything in common. Selling their possessions and goods, they gave to everyone as he [or she] had need. Every day they continued to meet together in the temple courts. They broke bread in their homes and ate together with glad and sincere hearts, praising God and enjoying the favor of all the people. And the Lord added to their number daily those who were being saved.*

The church was taking shape through some profound shared activities. The power of the Holy Spirit not only brought forgiveness of sin in Jesus' name and powerful spiritual gifts as seen in Acts 2, but also a depth of community unmatched before or since! Many people I know respond to this passage with the immediate defense of why they choose not to live this way — or simply cannot because of the differences in modern lifestyle.

My response continues to be the same: I want to understand and experience the depth of grace and power in Christ's love that would enable me to be willing to share all that I am and all that I have with reckless abandon! Something amazing began in those days of the early gatherings of believers.

While working in the former Soviet Union on eighteen different occasions in a span of ten years, I observed something that has profoundly changed me. Most Russian believers with whom I work have very little materially, yet I find that they share almost everything they have without question. When you are a brother or sister in Christ, you share. So, I would fly to Moscow and then work and live with Russians who have nothing and yet share everything; then I would get on an airplane again and fly home to Christians who have everything — and often struggle with sharing much at all.

At times I found myself crying on those return trips. It just did not make sense. At first, I thought the Russians were so open because of what they had learned under Communism, and that might be partly true. But there is no doubt that the main reason is the power of Christ's love sanctifying these believers, who freely share because they see it modeled by Jesus and the early church in Acts 2:42-47 and 4:31-37. These Russian Christians are relationally rich in Christ and model it by their sharing.

Another name for New Testament believers is *hagioi,* or saints, which actually relates directly to the just-mentioned concept of being sanctified in the Holy Spirit. Literally, Christians are the "made holy ones," those who understand that in Christ they are broken, sinful people who are made holy and righteous before God.[7] There is no need to impress others, to seek my worth or value in something or someone else, or to try to position myself as more important or higher than another. Holiness is something only God can create in the Christian life. Other saints are just like me, and so it is clear that, in Christ, the playing field is level for all of us — for all of life. This is yet another argument against the ladder mentality.

*Koinonia*, the word for fellowship, is another important concept that reflected early church life. The fellowship of the Spirit truly provided a vital connection between the individual believer and the group. From the start, it was clear that Christians did not grow as individuals in isolation. They were designed to grow in tandem, with "one another," a common New Testament phrase. "The creation of genuine fellowship is an integral part of the work of the Holy Spirit.... The church provides the context for spiritual growth by sharing together a fellowship which is at once the *gift* of the Spirit and the *environment* in which He may operate."[8]

> In Christ, the playing field is level for all of us — for all of life. This is yet another argument against the ladder mentality.

It took me a long time to understand that fellowship among Christians is not just a feeling of pleasure that comes by association with other believers or even from spending time with like-minded people. It is not something that we can manufacture. We are not just an organization of people that happens to be Christian.[9] Fellowship is truly a spiritual depth of unity and love that is created by the Holy Spirit. I am quite confident that those observing first-century *koinonia* did not have to be told this!

I am part of a men's small group through our church, City on a Hill in Albuquerque, New Mexico, where we are watching one man become very inquisitive about the things of God. Watching the Christians that make up the group has fascinated him to no end. He knows without question that something beyond the natural flow of friendship is going on in our midst. In fact, one of the other men in our group recently made a decision to follow Jesus, and the "fellowship of the Holy Spirit" among us found even greater depth — amazing to each of us supposedly more mature believers in the group!

While traveling in southern Russia several years ago, I experienced this supernatural reality of *koinonia* with a group of men that I trained in Rostov-on-Don - but this time in brand-new relationships, not long-term. I spent five days training this group of six men, with my translator alongside because of my inability to teach in Russian. We spent twelve hours a day together, eating meals, dialoguing about biblical concepts and their application for each of us. I stayed with one of the brothers, and we had casual time together as a part of each day. They loved showing me a different part of Rostov at any opportunity.

Something happened during that week, even with the liability of working through a translator. The Holy Spirit created a fellowship and a unity among us that was so much greater than five days shared together by six men. I will never forget the day I went to the train station for the 22-hour return trip to Moscow. Everyone came to the train station with me!

At first, I thought that most of them came because the train station was on their way home. But it turned out that they brought me to the train station all together because that is what you do for your brother. They also gave me a precious gift — a small malachite (semi-precious stone) box that none of them could have afforded to purchase individually. They gave me the gift, we cried and hugged, and then I slowly got on the train.

Once aboard, I hurried to my seat for one last look out the window at my brothers. For a few short minutes, I felt like the apostle Paul weeping with the elders as he left Ephesus. It was an experience I shall never forget. Such wealth of relationship is something only God could create.

All of our first three strategic words bring renewed depth to the fourth — a notion understood and practiced during the first century A.D. The word *oikos* means "household" or "extended family relationships." Chapter 2 introduces this key word through both Peter's and Paul's references to how the primary household relationships — husband/wife, parent/child, master/slave, and believer/unbeliever — were dramatically affected by the new fellowship of the Spirit.

How central is this word in understanding biblical relationships? It is the root of the word for God's economy mentioned earlier in Ephesians 3:2, *oikonomian.* This "economy of God's grace" has relationships at the core of its meaning. Our common understanding of the word *economy* relates to financial systems or the production of goods and services. Actually the word also can literally mean "the management of one's household." God's desire in his economy of grace — the managing of his household — is to put all things in order within his *oikos*, his household.[10] Relationships are on the top of God's list.

This new idea of Christian community, the household of God, reminds us that life is all about relationships. This principle of the primacy of extended family life was true then, and continues to be true today worldwide. "In every culture in the world, the intimacy of oikos connections is considered to be sacred. The Chinese have a special word for close friendships.... In Argentina, [there is] a gourd and metal tube with holes on one end for the drinking of mate' tea — a most intimate *oikos* custom."[11]

When I began to train national Christian leaders in their own countries, I was full of content! I was a "master trainer" with impeccable Christian credentials from the U.S., with great biblical vision and clear principles. I thought I knew what would work in their settings. I had a clear picture of what my desired results were, and how my prepared curriculum of material would help these first generation leaders effect changes in the Christian movement in their countries.

However, a funny thing happened on the way to my training objectives. I discovered that the Russians, the Kazakhs, and the Tamil-speaking Indians were not applying the principles I was giving them. It turns out that I did not yet have "right relationships." As a teacher, I learned over the next several trips that content presented without relationship brought little learning and no fruit in application. I could not get even a fair hearing no matter how great were the principles I was teaching!

As I returned for the third and fourth and fifth times, something noteworthy began to happen with those brothers and sisters I had come to train. Suddenly people began to listen to me and to apply the biblical principles. I was beginning to understand that the primacy of relationships was significantly different from the individualistic U.S. culture from which I came. This recognition caused me to work harder on such basic things as learning people's names and speaking to them by name as soon as possible. I also began to ask about their family and background.

Growing relational depth began to result in dramatically increased impact. When I would work with a new group represented by one of the people I had already worked with a number of times, my student and friend would say, "This man is my friend. Listen to him and trust him." Their words were similar to those Paul offered in Romans 16:1-2 about Phoebe: " I commend to you our sister Phoebe. ... I ask you to receive her in the Lord ... for she has been a great help to many people, including me."

Suddenly I had the complete attention of the whole group of new nationals! These longer-term relationships opened the doors to many more leaders and groups. I even changed my style of teaching to allow for much more personal interaction. After introducing a new biblical idea, I learned that both Russians and Kazakhs would talk about it in the group until everyone got it, and then they would be quiet. Working through curriculum content became a relational process as well.

I was beginning to understand cultures where the key for doing business or creating change was relationship — not money or position or

power or education. I had no position or power or value without relationship. The depth of this truth was mind-boggling! The Kazakhs even
began to call me "the American who remembers our names" because
they realized I wanted to be their friend and not just their teacher.

It no longer was about content alone,
information presented by the master teacher
with all the answers. The content had to be
wrapped in relational clothing, or it would
not be received. "Kinship now required a
shared humility and eliminated a jostling for
position."[12] Suddenly, Jesus' words in John

> **The content had to be
> wrapped in relational
> clothing, or it would
> not be received.**

15: 15 — calling his disciples friends — began to have tremendous significance. It is all about relationships in ways that I had never before
comprehended.

This 21st century illustration gives us a real clue as to the centrality
of *oikos* relationships in the first century. The Christian household
passages in Ephesians 5:21-6:10, Colossians 3:18-4:1, and 1 Peter 2:13-
3:16 reveal how dramatically the gospel was changing the nature of
primary relationships! This household of God would reveal the fellowship of the Holy Spirit by living out loving, grace-filled relationships. And
this is the model that would draw people to Jesus: a depth of love
portrayed in marriages, families, and work relationships. "Such affilia-
tions were intrinsic to ... the concept of the church as the household of
God."[13]

Pause for a moment and give thought to this possibility: Do you see
why, if you wanted to thwart God's economy — his grace-filled plans to
reach the world — it would make sense to establish a ladder-climbing
mentality as a primary tactic? That indeed is a primary scheme of the
enemy! Would it not be a brilliant strategy to encourage Christians to
give priority to objectives or position or wealth as more important than
relationship? And how about working to break down the fabric of relationships at every level in one's culture? The "divide and conquer"
model has been used with great success in battles everywhere.

If indeed God has structured the world to experience his grace and
his forgiveness primarily through his household of relationships, then
such a two-pronged plan to tear apart the primary relationships of life
would make perfect sense. The ladder mentality so often encourages us
to seek the end result or the higher position or the greater wealth.
However, God appears to be much more interested in the process of
relationships along the way — whatever the goal or end result.

## The Body of Christ: the Community Becomes Organic

As we have seen, the amazing thing about Christian community is that it is more than just great fellowship among like-minded people. It is the household of God and the fellowship of the Holy Spirit, to note direct identification with two persons of the Trinity. We now address the third person of the Trinity. The most common word or phrase used for the early church in the New Testament is the *soma christou*, the body of Christ.

Before we look more personally at the body of Christ, note that we now have language of community that involves all three persons of the Trinity. That should not surprise us, since the Father, Son, and Holy Spirit portray the very essence of community and relationship. God models it before we experience it! According to Eugene Peterson, "Trinity understands God as three-personed: Father, Son, and Holy Spirit, each 'person' in active communion with the others. We are given an understanding of God that is the most emphatically personal and interpersonal".[14] And Leonard Boffo writes, "The Trinity is the model for each and every community: while individuality is respected, the community emerges through communion and mutual self-surrender."[15]

While I make just these several references to this important reality, it is crucial in any discussion about the nature of Christian community. Excellent resources are available to look more deeply at this amazing spiritual reality.[16] It sets the foundation for understanding the nature and function of the body of Christ, the subject to which we now turn.

Here we begin to grasp the full reality of the church as the living presence of Jesus Christ revealed through Christians, the individual members of his body. Here we begin to understand the interdependence, the functionality, and the fundamental unity that are all parts of this ongoing presence of Jesus through the power of the Holy Spirit. Here we have the opportunity to comprehend the true organic nature of this life-giving body. "This metaphor expresses more graphically than anything else the essential unity between Christ and his church, and also between members of his church."[17]

Jesus fulfilled important Old Testament practices. He became the last sacrifice for sin, fulfilling the need for blood sacrifice for sin. He became our high priest, as seen in the book of Hebrews, and now, as his body, we become the priesthood of all believers. Through Jesus, no longer did the Israelites have to go to the temple to find God, but now the Holy Spirit would come and reside in every believer. And the whole body would become God's holy temple, our being built together to become a place where God lives by his Spirit.[18]

Both Jesus, in his human body, and the organic body of Christ were designed by God to fulfill his purposes in his economy of grace. Paul defines this reality in Ephesians 1:22-23:

> And God placed all things under his [Jesus'] feet and
> appointed him to be head over everything for the church,
> which is his body, the fullness of him who fills everything in
> every way.

The Greek word for body, *soma*, describes the unity of anything that is made up of various members.[19] But this body obviously is more than just the sum of its parts. It is the whole presence of God in the world and for the world. As Ralph Neighbor writes:

> "Christ first dwelled within the body shaped by the Father in
> the womb of Mary. His ministry now continues though the new
> body, which replaced the first one. That new body would have
> all the faculties and resources of a human body, plus all the
> eternal power and reality of the Godhead."[20]

**The Body of Christ Described.** The most astonishing part of this, though, is that you and I are integral parts of what is described here. We are the body of Christ! Let's take a literary walk through Paul's rendition of the organic body of Jesus, using portions of his words in 1 Corinthians 12:12-29 for greater insight:

> The body is a unit, though it is made up of many parts; and
> though its parts are many, they form one body. So it is with
> Christ. (12:12)

It appears that a Christian is an individual part of the body, yet is organically tied to all others in the body of Jesus. Even though spread all over the world, rich or poor, Asian or African or Anglo, president or pilot, janitor or jockey, handicapped or Olympic medal winner, we are all his unified body, his church, his household, his fellowship in the Holy Spirit!

> Now the body is not made up of one part but of many. If a foot
> should say, "Because I am not a hand, I do not belong to the
> body," it would not for that reason cease to be part of the
> body. (12:14-15)

You most certainly can try to act like you are separate from other Christians, but the reality is that you and I are inextricably tied to one another; that is, we can try to disentangle ourselves from other believers, but it just does not work. Our unity is an organic, spiritual reality by God's economic design. We were truly made for each other.

> If the whole body were an eye, where would the sense of hearing be? If the whole body were an ear, where would the sense of smell be? But in fact God has arranged the parts in the body, every one of them, just as he wanted them to be. If they were all one part, where would the body be? (12:17-19)

Each of us can try to decide what parts of the body we want to be, but attempting such will simply not work. God is the composer and arranger of this organic masterpiece, and he intentionally designed the body just like he wanted it to be. This reminds me of why it never worked when early in my Christian life I tried to be just like Tim (see chapter 1). God designed you to be you and me to be me. And the body of Christ would become a real mess if all of us tried to be just one or two of the so-called favorite parts. Paul speaks to that very subject:

> The eye cannot say to the hand, "I don't need you!" And the head cannot say to the feet, "I don't need you!" On the contrary, those parts of the body that seem to be weaker are indispensable, and the parts that we think are less honorable we treat with special honor. And the parts that are unpresentable are treated with special modesty, while our presentable parts need no special treatment. But God has combined the members of the body and given greater honor to the parts that lacked it, so that there would be no division in the body, but that its parts should have equal concern for each other. (12:21-25)

The body of Christ is also the great leveler. There really are no ladders in the body of Christ. In fact, the one to be lifted up or encouraged is actually the one who is hurting or has special needs.

God's economy revealed in this organic body is an amazing part of the world He has designed! Christian Schwarz, developer of Natural Church Development, says it this way: "One of the greatest miracles of God's creation is the interdependence of its parts, from the minutest microorganisms to the most magnificent stars. Viewing a phenomenon in the context of its manifold relationships rather than in isolation is what the Scriptures call 'wisdom.'"[21]

In the central Asian country of Kyrgyzstan I experienced this organic sense of unity and interdependence in an extraordinary way. While having supper together with ten or eleven people, we sat outdoors on traditional Kyrgyz padded pillows around in a circle. Each portion of the meal was served, and we just sat and ate and talked for several hours before I noticed how much time had passed. Someone asked a question about spiritual gifts, and I responded, and another brother pulled out his Bible and made several references. No one stood up to teach. Some asked questions, and others around the circle responded until it was quiet. Then another question or passage on gifts would be referenced and again we would learn together. Several more hours passed. Time had no importance as long as the relational interaction continued, a common occurrence in Kyrghyz and other central Asian cultures.

Finally it was time to go home. Such is the nature of *oikos*, or household life in the body of Christ! We Kyrghyz and Russians and Americans were all together, not aware of our differences, but rather became organically unified without thinking about it. There was a naturalness to that time, but also a supernaturalness. God was among us through his Spirit and gave us unity, depth of insight, and shared ministry one to another. "Our joy comes from our sharing in the divine grace and peace that creates and holds us in *koinonia.*"[22]

**Jesus Portrays Body Life.** Some have wondered why Jesus did not use this same body life language in a fashion similar to Paul. I think his reasons are quite clear. Jesus was himself, in his body, while in the form of his humanity. There was no need to talk about his body when his life and actions were modeling the very body life that we would experience later in the power of the Holy Spirit.

Jesus created true community for his followers. Consider the following facts:

- He lived with his disciples for three years, eating, drinking, and sleeping with them.

- He consistently modeled a lifestyle of love and servanthood.

- Despite his disciples' episodes of egotism, petty jealousies, and ladder climbing, he showed them the model of servanthood — even as one with full authority of God the Father.

- He washed their feet and even asked them to pray for him.

- Although he was their Lord and Master, he called them friends, and openly shared his life and kingdom purposes with them.

- He allowed no pecking order, as shown in an early attempt at ladder climbing by James and John.

- The focus of his significant time with the twelve in the upper room was unity.

- When he returned after his resurrection, he appeared to this group alone several times.

As Neighbor writes, "By living with 12 men, God in human flesh made a clear statement about how community develops. While thousands pressed him from every side, he chose to be with one cell of life."[23] The King of kings and Lord of lords provided clear guidance on his strategy. He chose relationship over earthly kingdom, community over comfort, relational investing to the point of sacrifice over building earthly security of any kind, and shared ministry over individual greatness. His ministry period was a sacrificial but powerful three years.

## Being Built Together

In God's economy of grace, it is not only what we are in Christ, but also what we are still in process of becoming. And, since his economy is lived out fully in the context of community, what biblical pictures can help us to grasp this reality? What does this plan of God's look like as we move forward even today? The Apostle Paul again helps us. Ephesians 2:19-22 not only summarizes some insights explored in this chapter, but also brings focus to what the body of Christ is still, to this day, in the process of becoming by the organic power of the Holy Spirit. First let us consider verses 19-20:

> **Consequently, you are no longer foreigners and aliens, but fellow citizens with God's people and members of God's household, built on the foundation of the apostles and prophets, with Christ Jesus himself as the chief cornerstone.**

It is clear that God's economy of grace given to Paul (see Ephesians 3:2) has created a new place for many to live. No matter if from another family or socio-economic class or country or race, in Christ we all now belong to God and are members of His *oikos*. And this household is not built on just any base, but on the foundational work of the prophets and the apostles, with Jesus himself as the cornerstone:

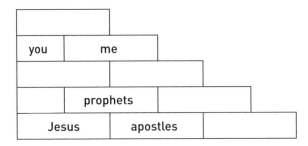

God has drawn us into his household, where we have become the body of Christ, a dynamic, interconnected group of believers worldwide who have the opportunity to experience the *koinonia*, or fellowship, of the Holy Spirit. God has made us for the very purpose of relationship with him, and now we live with Him and with one another in the dwelling he has "fitly framed together,"[24] with the prophets and the apostles laying out the early stages of God's house, with Jesus as the cornerstone — the one who holds everything else together, as Paul affirmed earlier in Ephesians 1:23. Paul continues in Ephesians 2:21-22.

> In him the whole building is joined together and rises to become a holy temple in the Lord. And in him you too are being built together to become a dwelling where God lives by his Spirit.

Many of us, when looking at a new house, office building, or skyscraper, tend to look at the whole building — the creative results of much planning and hard labor. Others of us want to look at the general schematics of how it was built, then go as deep into such understanding as our knowledge of construction and engineering will allow us. Either way we often are intrigued by the workmanship of what has been crafted. How was it put together, piece by piece, and how did the architects understand the issues of stress points and angles and weight-bearing load issues? How did the workers all understand just exactly what part each was to play in the completion of the building, floor by floor, walls and ceilings, windows and doors?

The book *To Engineer Is Human* told about a poorly designed bridge called the Tacoma Narrows Bridge. It was built in such a way that it could not handle the extreme tension put on the structural supports by the winds coming through the narrows. The result? The bridge began to fall apart and had to be torn down. Ever since then I have wondered about such questions about the design and workmanship of buildings and other structures. Poor planning, ill-conceived design, mismanaged organization, improper materials — all such things have tremendous impact on any building project.

In this dwelling under God's construction, though, we are safe. God is the architect of this building and has been from the beginning. He has prepared it with his economy of grace in mind and has put all of the parts in place just as he determined. All the stones that will be used in the building — those of us in the body of Christ — are living stones chosen by God to fulfill his purposes in the building.[25]

For what purposes did he originally build this building? Paul gives a hint in his wording: "the whole building is joined together and rises to become a holy temple in the Lord." The temple was the headquarters for worship for the people of Israel, so now, in God's new economy, this group of people forming the new holy temple that he is building know that it is a place of worship. God continues to desire the praises of His people, and will until the end of time — as the book of Revelation so clearly reveals. Thus, worship is a key activity in God's household, now and forever among his people. In a related sense, it will also be a place of the personal, abiding presence of the Lord, since we are his new temple. It will be the place where God lives by his Spirit.

Finally, it is a living building, not yet fully constructed: "you too are being built together..." As the body of Christ, we are still very much in process of organically being built together. The master architect is still developing his workmanship, an idea noted several verses earlier in Ephesians 2:10, and he is still creating and renewing and changing and growing his body. This new temple is God's household, the place he will live with his people. It is his new temple, from which the praises of his people in worship will continue to pour out. It is also the place where he will continue to live and move and have his way among us, the inter-woven stones.[26]

This is the same idea portrayed in Ephesians 4:13-16 — that of his people's organic, ongoing life in the Spirit. While the next chapter looks at this passage more thoroughly, take note here of one important factor: The body of Christ is the living, breathing presence of Jesus, growing and maturing in unity as each part in the body plays its God-designed role. God is building a temple in and through his people, where he will be worshiped and have the freedom to work his purposes. There is still a major building phase that is an ongoing part of the body of Christ!

# Conclusion

Howard Snyder, in his powerful book *The Problem of Wineskins* writes, "When the local church is structured after an instititutional model ... spiritual gifts are replaced by aptitude, education and technique."[27] Sometimes, on things that are specifically related to the working of God's economy of grace and the building of his body, he just does not need our help!

Snyder also has serious concerns about church buildings, that is, the physical structures themselves: "Church buildings are a witness to our immobility. Church buildings are a witness to our inflexibility. Church buildings are a witness to our lack of fellowship."[28] God decided to use his people as the basic structure of his church. He determined to make the gathering of the body of Christ the place where he lives and also the place where they worship him in spirit and truth. And then he made the people to be the ones who continue, to this day, to carry on the full ministry of Jesus Christ. By his design, he gave each of them specific and powerful ministry functions, as we shall soon see. Such workmanship is what will continue to drive the ongoing construction of his "being built together" dwelling. Why? So that he can continue to live and move and have his way among us, to his praise and glory.

Margaret J. Wheatley asks:

Why do organizations feel lifeless? Why do projects so often take so long, develop ever-greater complexity, yet too often fail to achieve any truly significant results? Why does progress, when it appears, so often come from unexpected places, or as a result of surprises or synchronistic events that our planning had not considered."[29]

A long-time friend from a mission agency with whom I have worked for many years recently shared a disturbing assessment: "The organization pushes the organic move of the Spirit to the edge of priority, usually to organizationally solidify itself in its already established fields."[30] His main fear was that the Spirit might be squelched and that new open doors where God is clearly leading would be closed due to organizational priorities.

However, perhaps God does not need as much organizational and strategic help as we have thought over the past years. Most likely he is particularly interested in our becoming more aware of his strategies through his organic design.

What, then, is the role of the leader in this life-giving, dynamic body?

# Chapter 4 endnotes

[1] Durant, Will and Ariel. *The Lessons of History* (NY: Simon & Schuster, 1968), p 45.

[2] Snyder, Howard A. *Liberating the Church* (Downers Grove, IL: Intervarsity Press, 1983), pp 51-52.

[3] Harrison, Norman. His Very Own: *Paul's Epistle to the Ephesians* (Chicago: Bible Institute Colportage Association, 1930), p 80.

[4] Sallee, Larry. Quote from short article about his "Seed and Light" Ministry. For more information, contact Larry at *Larry1702@aol.com*.

[5] Ladd, George Eldon. *Theology of the New Testament* (Grand Rapids: Eerdmans, 1974), p 351.

[6] Ephesians 2:21-22.

[7] Ladd, p 544.

[8] Snyder, Howard A. *The Problem of Wineskins* (Downers Grove, IL: Intervarsity Press, 1975), p

[9] Ladd, p 543.

[10] Snyder, *The Problem of Wineskins*, p 56.

[11] Neighbour, Jr., Ralph. *Where Do We Go from Here?* (Houston: Touch Publications, 2000), p 134.

[12] Minear, Paul S. *Images of the Church in the New Testament* (Philadelphia: John Knox Press, 1960), p 171.

[13] Watson, David. *I Believe in the Church* (Grand Rapids, MI: Eerdmans, 1978), p 97.

[14] Peterson, Eugene. *Christ Plays in Ten Thousand Places* (Grand Rapids: Eerdmans, 2005), pp 44-45.

[15] Boff, Leonardo. *Holy Trinity, Perfect Community* (Maryknoll, NY: Orbis Books, 2000), p 53.

[16] In addition to the references in 13 and 14, consider *Richard of St. Victor: Book Three of the Trinity* by Grover A, Zinn, editor, and *Mere Christianity* by C. S. Lewis, p 127.

[17] Ephesians 2:22.

[18] Watson, p 97.

[19] Snyder, *The Problem of Wineskins*, p 57.

[20] Neighbour, p 121

[21] Schwarz, Christian. *Color Your World with Natural Church Development* (St. Charles, IL: ChurchSmart Resources, 2005), p 92.

[22] Shults, LeRon & Sondage, Steven. *The Faces of Forgiveness* (Grand Rapids, MI: Baker Academic, 2003), p 205.

[23] Neighbour, p 119.

[24] Bruce, F.F. *The Epistle to the Ephesians* (Toronto: Fleming H. Revell Company, 1961), p 58.

[25] 1 Peter 2:4.

[26] Liefield, Walter L. *Ephesians* (Downers Grove: Intervarsity Press, 1997), p 72.

[27] Snyder, *The Problem of Wineskins*, p 130.

[28] Ibid, pp 70-71.

[29] Wheatley, Margaret J. *Leadership and the New Science* (San Francisco: Berrett-Koehler Publishers, 1999), p 3.

[30] Quote from an anonymous friend in an international ministry.

# CHAPTER FIVE

## Leadership Re-Engineered: Being a Good Steward

Today I repent before you, brothers and sisters. I release control as the leader. Up to this day, I have held every important leadership function close to my heart so that I could be important. I release that power today. No more will I be seen as a great leader among the Kazakhs, but as one who helps others accept Jesus and find their places of service.
    Timurzhan — "chief" Kazakh in a training group
    Almaty, Kazakhstan, April, 2000

Each one should use whatever gift he or she has received to serve others, as good stewards (*oikonomos*) of the grace of God in its various forms. If anyone speaks, speak as if speaking the very words of God. If anyone serves, serve with the strength that God provides, so that in all things God may be praised through Jesus Christ. To him be the glory and the power for ever and ever. Amen.
    1 Peter 4:10-11

What strikingly clear pictures we have of the context for God's economy of grace in the church. We are the household of God, the fellowship of the Holy Spirit and the organic, living body of Jesus Christ in the world of the new millennium.

So then, how does the leader fit into this dynamic group of Christians? It is time to take a comprehensive look at this concept in the

New Testament.

However, there is no broad overview of the leader or leadership idea in the New Testament. There is no thorough treatment of the leader as an important player in the ministry of the body of Jesus. There are studies of Moses, Nehemiah, and David from the Old Testament, and you are welcome to find those resources and read them if you like. Our purpose here, though, is to identify the nature of leadership as it relates to God's household, the body of Christ, and the fellowship of the Holy Spirit.

In the New Testament world, we find new wine created through the death and resurrection of Jesus. It takes the form of the Spirit of God residing inside each individual believer from Pentecost forward. From there, God creates a powerful, unified fellowship of Christians who are designed to change the world through the web of *oikos*, extended relationships that he has prepared. That is, within God's new economy of grace, he has engineered a living, organic body that cannot be held within organizational constraints.

What words does Scripture use to describe direction and guidance for the body of Christ? The word leadership is used in the New Testament, but its scope is very limited. In Romans 12:8, the Greek word for leadership, *proisameno*, is listed as one of the spiritual gifts given to believers. Look at the word in context:

> We have different gifts, according to the grace given us. If a man's gift is prophesying, let him use it in proportion to his faith. If it is serving, let him serve; if it is teaching, let him teach; if it is encouraging, let him encourage; if it is contributing to the needs of others, let him give generously; *if it is leadership, let him govern diligently*; if it is showing mercy, let him do it cheerfully. [Romans 12: 6-8; emphasis added]

The gift of leadership is one of the gifts given in the economy of God's grace. It is one among a number of gifts of the Holy Spirit described in this Romans passage, in 1 Corinthians 12, and in Ephesians 4. It has its place as one gift among a number of powerful gifts given to members of the body of Christ. There is no encouragement to attain this gift, or wording anywhere that would suggest that a special quality, power, or authority is given by God with this particular gift. As with other gifts, Paul says, if you have it, use it vigorously, that is, with great effort: *"if it is leadership, let him govern diligently"*

In 1 Thessalonians 5:12-13, Paul does encourage us to respect and hold in high regard those who "*are over us in the Lord*," but the word *leader* is not used here or in any other place of note in the rest of the New Testament. The gift of leadership is different than a position of oversight, or "one in authority." *Overseer, elder*, and *deacon* are words used for those in positions of authority, as noted in 1 Timothy 3 and Titus 1. The word *leader* is never used in this way.

Our desire here is to find what words are used to describe those who are in such positions of directing and guiding others in the body of Christ. If *leader* is not described as a primary word related to *the* directing and managing of ministry in the body of Christ, what words are used? As we uncover these words, we will also find concepts that help us understand the nature and role of New Testament overseers and elders as well.

## God's Household Managers

An important reference to the qualifications of overseers, found in Titus 1:7, brings us to the first significant word for guiding the body of Christ. "Since an overseer is entrusted with God's work, he must be blameless." The literal Greek translation is "Since an overseer is God's steward." This word "steward," *oikonomos*, means that an overseer is "God's household manager." He or she is the one relationally entrusted with the "household work" of God. Keeping in mind what we learned in chapter 4, does it surprise you that our first biblical expression for leaders in body life is cast in relational language? What is most interesting, though, is that we return to the same root word as that for "economy, or administration," *oikonomia*, and "household," *oikos*! Thus, God's economy of grace includes the building up of God's household, now with God's stewards, or relationship managers, as key players entrusted to help encourage and build up the body of Christ.

Other references to *oikonomos* shed further light on the significance of this idea of stewardship. Luke 12:42-44 says that the *oikonomos*, the steward, will be given oversight for the master's household (*oikos*). The steward is given responsibility for the entire household after he shows himself to be faithful and wise. The steward is truly the one entrusted by the master to bring to full capacity all of the master's resources. That includes the work of the master's staff — the workers themselves and all of their functions. In 1 Corinthians 4:1, we see the "stewardship of resources" concept given spiritual meaning. "So then, men ought to regard us as servants of Christ, as those entrusted with [as stewards of] the secret things of God." Paul calls himself a household manager, one who must prove himself faithful, as verse 2 reveals. The steward is one who faithfully manages the resources of God, whether it is grace, truth, relationships, or serving functions.

Why would stewardship of his resources be important to God? It is no wonder! Since God is the "supreme householder,"[1] it is his household of which we are a part as the church, the body of Christ. "The church is far from being a family under the fatherly care of some mission; it is God's own family."[2] He desires faithful stewardship of his household, both its people and functional resources, because it is his economy of grace.

I attended Tarkio College, a small liberal arts college in the Midwest. During my sophomore year, I discovered three freshmen who wanted to go deeper in their Christian lives. I did what I thought every growing Christian would do; I went to my pastor, Jack Wineman. He was meeting with a group of my peers and me in a weekly Bible study that was truly timely in my spiritual growth. Certainly he could do that for these three guys. But he said no. Instead he encouraged me to come alongside these three guys. I told him I didn't feel qualified. I was just a young, budding Christian.

"Who understood their need to grow?" Jack asked me.

"Well, I guess I did."

"Who took immediate steps to provide a way for them to actively go deeper in their faith?" Jack continued.

"I guess I did that too."

"Paul, these guys know you and trust you relationally. And you are a great encourager. I have a workbook on discerning God's best for one's life that you could take them through week to week. If they ask you questions you cannot answer, tell them you don't know but you will find out by the next week. As long as you are one step ahead of them, they will be just fine with the process."

It turned out that Jack was right! They did not need him, the official pastor. They just needed another Christian, someone they knew and trusted, to come alongside and use his gifts to help them grow. I could do that. I offered to meet with them, and they were overjoyed. We each got a copy of the workbook, and I asked each one to come prepared — and they did, each one, faithfully, every week.

I encouraged them a lot, and they all — we all — grew in the Lord by leaps and bounds. They did ask questions that I could not answer, and I did just what Jack said and told them I would find the answer by the next week. There were several times that I had to go back to Jack and ask for help, but he appreciated that and encouraged me all the more.

This was my first real experience as a Christian where I discovered that the stewardship of relationships is a major part of God's strategy. I understood later that Jack also saw this as an opportunity for me to use my spiritual gift of exhortation, already apparent in my early discipleship. By challenging me to use my gifts in my relationships, he gave me my first lesson in being a faithful steward of God's grace.

**Learn to Be Who You Are, Where You Are.** One final stewardship passage leads us to an excellent summary of this idea. In fact, 1 Peter 4:10-11 is where I began to grasp the true reality of spiritual leadership in the body of Christ. These words also revealed for me God's strategy for reaching the world, and how each of us participates fully in that process, no matter who we are or how we fit in his household.

> Each one should use whatever gift he or she has received to serve others, as faithful stewards of the manifold grace of God. If anyone speaks, he or she should speak as if speaking the very words of God. If anyone serves, he or she should do it with the strength God provides, so that in all things God may be praised through Jesus Christ. To Him be the glory and the power for ever and ever.

We are called to be faithful stewards of God's grace. By the very meaning of the word *steward* we know that, in the first place, we are to be faithful in our relationships — each to our respective households. That is, we are to be committed to those people whom God has entrusted to us. Remember: it is his economy, so he even has the relationships prepared for us. We are also to be household managers of God's grace in its many forms, that is, stewards of our spiritual gifts. In fact, the first part of the passage now makes perfect sense: "Each one should use whatever gift he or she has received to serve others as good stewards of the manifold grace of God."

In the New Testament Greek, the word for spiritual gift has *grace* as its root. "Spiritual gift," *charisma*, has the root word of *charis*, or grace. That is why in every spiritual gifts passage in the New Testament you will find the word *grace* alongside spiritual gifts. Out of God's grace come the gifts of the Spirit. Also, both words have the root word of *char*, meaning joy. Using your spiritual gifts, given as a portion of God's grace personally to you, results in joy abounding!

Here is how it works. We have been saved by grace, a free gift from God and not something we can earn for ourselves, as Ephesians 2:8-9 states. The first thing that happens in the next verse, 2:10, is that by God's grace, each of us becomes "the workmanship of God, created in Christ Jesus to do good works." What does that workmanship look like? It looks like the spiritual gifts we are given: "But to each one of us grace has been given as Christ apportioned it." (Ephesians 4: 7) If you continue to read this passage (4:7-13), you will see that Paul is indeed talking about spiritual gifts.

Thus, Peter calls us to be good stewards of God's grace, faithful in both our relationships and in the using of our spiritual gifts. You can learn to be *who you are* through your spiritual gifts, and learn to be *right where you are* in the relationships that God has given to you. Living out the Spirit-driven power of our gifts is yoked with living out your relationships — and God gave you both parts!

**The Centrality of Spiritual Gifts and Relationships in Acts 2.**
Subsequent chapters will further address 1 Peter. However, we now pause again to take note of something else of great substance. Just how important is this stewardship concept to biblical leadership?

Early in his ministry, Jesus spoke dramatically about his body: "Destroy this temple, and I will raise it again in three days."

Those were Jesus' words to the Jews in John 2:19. After his death, fulfilling this passage, he rose from the dead, and promised power from the Holy Spirit (Acts 1:8) before ascending into heaven. The new temple, Jesus' body of believers, is now to become a living organism, starting in Jerusalem as described in Acts 2.

The waiting huddle of Jesus' followers receive the power of the Spirit in two supernatural ways: (1) Spiritual gifts are released and people from many nations respond to the different supernatural tongues spoken, each into their own language; they also respond to Peter's Spirit-empowered preaching (Acts 2: 1-40). (2) This new "temple" of interwoven relationships, God's new household, is being built together into a place where God lives by His Spirit (Acts 2: 41-47; Ephesians 2: 22). Thus, this new organic body of Christ is life-giving and life-changing both in the power of the Spirit — spiritual gifts — and in the depth of relationships — community!

These are the same two areas where each of us is called to be a good steward in 1 Peter 4:10-11! It is no wonder that God calls each of us to act as stewards of our gifts and our relationships. We already know from chapter 4 how strategically important relationships are to God. His primary strategy is indeed a relational one. Now we are beginning to realize how important spiritual gifts are.

Did you know that, just as we have seen each person of the Trinity involved actively with the new community of believers, we will find the same thing to be true of spiritual gifts? In the New Testament, these are the only two situations where all three members of the Trinity are involved. The New Testament portrays Christians as the household of God, the body of Christ, and the fellowship of the Holy Spirit. With spiritual gifts, it is God who determines the gifts, Jesus who gives them, and the Spirit who empowers each gift.[3] This is foundational stuff, and all three persons of the Trinity are involved in both. No wonder God calls us to be faithful stewards!

Note also that the exercising of spiritual gifts and the profound changes in relationships that dominate Acts 2 actually become ongoing realities in the organic body of Christ. We see four major passages on the ministry of spiritual gifts and at least as many on household relationships (husband/wife, etc.) in the ongoing development of authentic fellowship in the Holy Spirit. God's economy of grace, from the beginning of this new body life, takes on these two important features, and our call is to be stewards of both of these areas in our Christian lives.

The leader is to be a good steward of God's grace in the relationships that God has prepared in his or her world. I spent many years trying to become the right kind of Christian leader — through college, seminary, and my early experience as a local church pastor. I tried to fit all the roles that I thought the pastor or Christian leader should fit. Through a new understanding of 1 Peter 4:10-11, at the five-year mark of my pastoral ministry, I discovered that I was free to be myself in Christ!

I finally realized why I did not fit well in a major part of my first traditional pastoral role. I was a horrible pastoral counselor, which was a major part of my job. (Even I would not have gone to myself for pastoral care or counseling!)   I was afraid of hospital visitation and nursing home ministry. But most of all, I came to understand that it was my job to release others to do ministry and not my responsibility to do all the ministry myself. My spiritual gifts are exhortation, leadership, and prophecy. I loved to help people discover their spiritual gifts, then equip and release them to play their parts in the body life. I had to leave the pastorate to fully act as steward of my gifts and my calling to work with leaders and teams in different cultures.

In the cross-cultural work I really began to grasp at a deeper level the centrality of relationships, as described in stories in each chapter so far. A brother in Kazakhstan brought me to this new depth of insight concerning the stewardship of relationships.

Adilet was a part of my first three trips into southeast Kazakhstan to train Kazakh pastors and other Christian leaders. Each time I came, he, several of his friends, and I grew closer, and a trust relationship was finally established toward the end of my third trip to this part of central Asia. Just before I left for home, Adilet came to me and said, "If I promise to bring you 200 of my family and friends from northern Uzbekistan to meet with you, would you come to my village and train them?" Because of our friendship, my automatic response was, "Of course!" I also saw this as a real opportunity to begin to share training responsibilities with Adilet. This would further affirm my helping to be a steward of his ministry of equipping and releasing others, even while I was doing the same.

Little did I know what an adventure I had gotten myself into! The next trip, I fulfilled my promise. My interpreter and I traveled eight hours west from Almaty, Kazakhstan, by train, then six hours south by car, finally to arrive in a small town near the southernmost point of Kazakhstan — a place where few Americans had gone up to this point in time. I quickly realized that few foreigners from *any* country had ever been there!

Our original plan was for us to cross the border into Uzbekistan, but the local Muslim government, just the week before, had stopped allowing Christians to congregate together. So all of Adilet's family and friends from a number of house fellowships in Uzbekistan came over the border, where we all poured into a Kazakh home that was big enough for us to gather for worship, fellowship, and teaching. Everyone sat on the floor, as is their custom, except for those who had to hang out the windows because it was so crowded. It felt as if we were in the early church, where believers crowded together in homes in excited anticipation of what God would do!

At this point I had my foundation-shaping realization about God's economic strategy administered through relationships. Chapter 4 briefly describes what happened next. Adilet said, "This is my friend and my mentor, Paul Ford. Listen to him." He had clearly said that before I came, as the excitement was obvious in the way people packed into that room — and then stayed as I taught and we talked until 1:30 in the morning, only to come back the next morning to finish our time together.

I had invested in Adilet, and that investment had born fruit into four other communities in northern Uzbekistan through this gathering. I had done nothing but work hard on building a friendship as I trained this brother. Such stewardship of people whom God gives to you can have an impact in places you might never expect.

What principle was realized? If I am faithful relationally with those whom God brings to me, and use my gifts as well, he will fulfill his kingdom purposes through that course of action. God will then extend the process outwardly into *oikos*, household relationships, in ways that I could never plan.

A second heart-felt realization came two days later in the village of Abai, named after a famous Kazakh poet. We stopped by a house church of believers, where there was another brother whom I had trained in Almaty years earlier, and who, with Adilet's help, also had become my trusted friend. As we finished meeting that day — the first day that Adilet had trained on spiritual gifts for a whole afternoon on his own, without my input — I was dumbstruck by a simple discovery. In five days, Adilet had never been farther than ten feet from me. When I first arrived in southern Kazakhstan, I noticed him saying goodbye to his wife, but did not think about it again until this later time in Abai. We ate together and he slept on the floor in the same room with my interpreter and me each night. He traveled by foot or by car wherever we went, always by my side. As he left to go home to Uzbekistan that last evening, this realization flooded in and I began to weep as we were saying goodbye.

I thought I had been the wise one who was being a good steward of my brother, training him and then encouraging him to use his gifts as I stepped aside. But all along, he was being a good steward relationally as well, knowing that we were in a militant Muslim area where it was not safe for me to be out on my own. Stewardship of gifts, stewardship of relationships, it all began to intertwine on this trip in a way that I never before experienced. Again, my Kazakh brothers taught me the secret things of God's economy even while I thought I was the teacher and the good steward!

Southern Kazakhstan offered incredible opportunity for training new leaders in the natural web of relationships within the *oikos*, or household. In the first-century household of God, "This context of effective stewardship also became the most natural way to train the next generation of leaders. What is their most important training? Learning to live in right relationships, first with family members but extending strategically out into one's sphere of relational influence."[4] Adilet used his gifts to train the Abai house church group with his younger partner in ministry, Shingiz, alongside. I saw the model for training the next generation of Kazakh believers develop before my very eyes — led by Adilet, not me.

This can happen wherever, we are intentional in our equipping and releasing of others. No wonder 1 Peter 4:10-11 ends with God receiving the praise and the glory. We are not smart enough to figure out this multi-layered process of stewardship on our own. "To him be the glory and the power forever and ever!"

Now I was starting to get the whole picture. As a Christian leader, I seek to be a steward of who I am through my spiritual gifts, while at the same time being a good steward of the relationships he gives me along the way. If I am faithful to be who I am, where I am, he will fulfill his purpose and give clarity to each step. Such is the functioning of his economy of grace.

## The Equipper

Ephesians 4:11-16 helps us articulate the nature of leadership in the New Testament, that of equipping or "preparing the saints for the work of ministry." It also matches spiritual gifting with relational body life unity, our now-familiar pair of New Testament concepts.

Prior to this passage Paul outlines the following pivotal concepts (which we have examined in this chapter and chapter 4):

- The church as the body of Christ is the fullness of Jesus in every way (Ephesians 1:22-23).

- Christians are saved by grace and through that grace have become the very workmanship of God  (2:8-10).

- In Christ, God has established his own household, which is a temple of these believers being built together to become a place where he lives by his Spirit (2:19-22).

- God has his own economy, the management of his grace in the world (3:2).

- The management of that grace includes spiritual gifts apportioned to each Christian by Jesus (4:7).

Before we continue, please note what follows in Ephesians 5, just beyond our focus in 4:11-16. In 5:21-6:9 we find detailed *oikos*, household guidelines, for living out our relationships in Christ! It is within this context, in the passages before and after, that Paul addresses the issues of how to encourage the body of Christ, and each member, to live out body life ministry in collective unity of relationships.

In God's economy of grace, this organic body where he lives among his people, we find his workmanship designed for his purposes. Through this dynamic fellowship we gain a glimpse of how the body of Christ is equipped by the body itself. Paul writes in Ephesians 4:

It was he [Jesus] who gave some to be apostles, some to be prophets, some to be evangelists, and some to be pastor and teachers, to prepare God's people for works of service, so that the body of Christ may be built up until we all reach unity in the faith and in the knowledge of the Son of God, and become mature, attaining to the whole measure of the fullness of Christ.

Then we will no longer be infants, tossed back and forth by the waves, and blown here and there by every wind of teaching and by the cunning and craftiness of men in their deceitful scheming. Instead, speaking the truth in love, we will in all things grow up into him who is the Head, that is, Christ. From him the whole body, joined and held together by every supporting ligament, grows and builds itself up in love, as each part does its work. (4:11-16)

**Equipped for Works of Service.** Jesus, the gift-giver, gives certain believers gifts that are to "equip, prepare, establish or strengthen" Christians for service to the Lord and to fellow humankind. The Greek word for these gifts is *katartidzo*.[5] The various interpretations of these gifts are many. For our purposes here, we know that each is a spiritual gift in its own right, whether or not it is a ministry office, and that each is a part of a larger set of gifts that is powerfully able in the Spirit to equip and release the saints for the work of ministry. I call these equipping gifts, which we will discuss in a larger context in chapter 6. According to F.F. Bruce, "The gifts enumerated in verse 11 do not monopolize the church's ministry; their function rather is to help and direct the church that all the members may perform for the good of the whole."[6]

Equipping is not to be equated with leading — at least from a biblical standpoint. The biblical priority is that the saints be prepared for ministry, not simply led. Today we have many Christians who are well led but have not been properly equipped for ministry, nor are they using their spiritual gifts in any way, shape, or form! In fact, many may not know what those gifts are.

Leading is one part of equipping the saints, as are exhorting, pastoring, evangelizing, teaching, prophesying, and other equipping-type spiritual gifts; however leading is not the whole of the process. There are real dangers of a ministry organized in a manner that gives a high position to the gift of leadership or one that makes leadership the only important role. I have been truly amazed over the past fifteen years at the number of Christians who admit, after a

> **Today we have many Christians who are well led but have not been properly equipped for ministry, nor are they using their spiritual gifts in any way, shape, or form!**

process of sober estimation, that they're projecting leadership as one of their spiritual gifts related directly to their own desire to be seen as important by others to move higher up the ladder of ministry.

Remember again: body life ministry is not primarily about leading well. It is more about functions related to equipping others (Ephesians 4: 12) and supporting others (4:16). This equipping and supporting language takes center stage in chapter 6. That chapter shows how clearly each word delineates a type of essential function in body life ministry.

Take note of Timurzhan's quote that opens this chapter. It was this reality of equipping versus his perception of leading that Timurzhan began to deal with on that spring day of 2000. He began to grasp that, whatever role he had as a leader in the body of Christ, his responsibility was to equip and release others to play their God-designed parts. He no longer had to control all the important functions for himself, and he stepped out with new insight and a different approach. Timurzhan is now using his own gifts – especially the gift of evangelism – first to release others into the body by accepting Christ and then to empower them to fulfill their gifted functions in the body. He is having impact as a steward of his gifts in the context of his relationships in a number of regions in Kazakhstan. God's economy of grace has empowered Timurzhan to be used powerfully as himself, just where he needs to be, in relationships. He has laid down the desire to be a great leader.

Peter writes, "Humble yourselves under the mighty hand of God, and in due time He will lift you up." (I Peter 5:6) Like Timurzhan, I spent much of my life seeking position to prove my worth and significance, something that I now know Jesus has already settled on the cross. And I, too, have discovered my gifts and am watchful for those relationships — past, present, and future — that God gives in the economy of his body life. We both have laid down any desire to raise ourselves up, knowing that God takes care of the positioning to fulfill the stewardship of his grace!

**Equipped for Body Unity and Maturity.** As each minister is prepared for individual and collective works of service, an amazing thing happens: the body of Christ grows and even builds itself up in love and truthful speaking. This is the part I missed in my preparation for ministry, and it appears that, with disunity, broken fellowship, and torn fabric in the body of Christ everywhere, that my situation is not unique. Look again at Ephesians 4:12-13: "...to prepare God's people for works of service so that the body of Christ may be built up until we all reach unity in the faith and in the knowledge of the Son of God, and become mature, attaining to the whole measure of the fullness of Christ."

For years I stopped paying attention after the "works of service" part. But now, as we have reviewed the nature of the church as relationally centered and relationally built up, we know that the passage is not complete without the part after "works of service." People learning to play their parts is essential — it is stated more clearly in verse 16 — but it is unity as the body of Christ that is the other essential part. It reminds us again why Jesus prayed for unity among all of his followers in John 20:19-26, and why Paul was so clear about the centrality of living in like-minded community in Philippians 2:1-6.

Living in unity, both in relationships and in functionally using our gifts, is in fact the only way we will come to maturity. It is the only way that we experience all that God has for us. No wonder Peter calls us to be stewards of the grace of God in both our gifts and our relationships! In true like-mindedness, Paul challenges us that we all be equipped for the same reasons — for body ministry and body unity. Why? Because that is how we come into the fullness of Christ, into true intimacy with God in the fellowship of the Holy Spirit. This is the nature of God's economy, the secret things he has for us in Christ!

We need the Lord to teach us how to do both of these stewardship functions in tandem! Paul knew of the challenges, no doubt, which is likely the reason for Ephesians 4:15-16. Speaking the truth in love is a key action, crucial in a world of broken relationships. Acting as supporting ligaments is another strategic action; this is what holds us together! And then Paul reiterates that each one is to play his or her functional, gifted, powerful part. None of these actions is optional; all are needed. No one can be inactive; everyone must participate. The unity, maturity and growth of the body of Christ depend upon these things.

## The Minister: The Last and Lowest Word

As described in chapter 3, the one common problem I have discovered worldwide is the problem of authoritarian leadership. It is a problem I have found to be particularly common in groups whose theology gives high position or "offices" to the spiritual gifts listed in Ephesians 4:11. It is the ultimate ladder-climbing attempt to take control of the body of Christ, of which Jesus is the only true head. As we look at the nature of Christian "ministers," note church growth researcher Christian Schwarz's invaluable insights on the nature of body life and the kind of leadership that works best for this organism:

> Outside the Christian realm there is this concept sometimes known as "guru leadership." Similar models can be found in Christian churches as well. Some people even uphold this concept as an especially effective growth principle — the guru leader with the great vision on one hand and the lay troops who willingly serve their leader as he fulfills his life dreams, on the other.
>
> Our research reveals that this could not be farther from the truth. Leaders of growing churches consider it one of their most important tasks to empower others. They equip, support, motivate, and mentor individuals to become all that God wants them to be.[7]

Biblical leaders need to understand that they are to be good stewards of both the people and the spiritual gifts given to them and around them. They understand that to equip and release others to play their body life parts is far more important than looking impressive as a leader!

We now turn to a final word that was used as New Testament language for the believers who served as stewards of grace and equippers of the saints. Note first that it appears that Jesus and Paul deliberately did not use religious leader language common in their day: priest, ruler, rabbi, and master. They did not want to portray Christians in authority as being in a special or privileged class.[8] They were not to be put in the same class as the authoritarian secular or religious leaders of the day.

This final word, used by both Jesus and Paul, is "minister," *diakonos*. According to Richard Niebuhr, "The word *diakonos* is a functional word meaning a person who renders acts of service to others, particularly waiting on tables. When Jesus said, 'I am among you as one who serves,' he is using this word."[9] Many times Paul called himself a minister of the gospel. There was no New Testament distinction between such ministry and leadership in the church.

In my life, the clearest embodiment of this servant model is a long-time partner in my overseas work, David Graffenberger. He oversees a ministry of evangelism and church planting in scores of cultures world-wide. He is tireless in his desire to see communities won for Christ everywhere he goes, whether in Indiana, Haiti, or India. This man is the only person with whom I have ever worked who models a humility that is no different when leading from the front than when serving from behind or below.

When we began to work together, as the younger brother and apprentice I expected that he would teach me how to lead. I observed in him attitudes and actions that were consistently aimed toward serving others, with no concern for his own position. As we began to spend more time together, he again surprised me. He asked if we could become accountability partners — the older and wiser with the younger novice - and share our weak areas so that we could pray for each other. He did teach me leadership: it was servanthood laced with true humility. He knew the One who served and resolutely followed his servant model.

Read Paul's words in Philippians 2:5-8 about the One who served:

Your attitude should be the same as that of Christ Jesus:
Who, being in very nature God,
did not consider equality with God something to be grasped,
but made himself nothing, taking the very nature of a servant,
being made in human likeness.
And being found in an appearance as a man
he humbled Himself and became obedient to death —
even death on a cross!

Now consider Jesus' words about authoritarian leadership:

"You know that the rulers of the Gentiles lord it over them and their high officials exercise authority over them. Not so with you. Instead, whoever wants to become great among you must be your servant, and whoever wants to be first must be your slave — just as the Son of Man did not come to be served, but to serve, and to give his life as a ransom for many." (Matthew 20: 25-28)

This same Jesus of whom Paul spoke, the one who defined greatness as servanthood, washed his disciples' feet and said, "Now that I, your Lord and Teacher, have washed your feet, you also should wash one another's feet. I have set you an example that you should do as I have done for you." (John 13: 14-15)

This should remove any final attempts at ladder climbing in the kingdom.

## Conclusion

If you want to study the formal leadership words given in passages like Titus 1 and 1 Timothy 3, that is, elders, deacons, bishops and overseers, many resources are available to you.[10] There are elders, deacons, bishops, and overseers in the body of Christ all over the world. However, whatever biblical words you use for spiritual leadership, be aware that three crucial concepts come into play for any leader in the church. God's economy of grace has made it so.

(1) It is essential that Christian leaders understand that they are *stewards* of God's grace-driven, powerful spiritual gifts and of their households of relationships. (2) It is strategic that leaders see themselves as *equippers* of body life gifting and relational unity. Finally (3), it is imperative that they realize they are true *ministers*, servants who serve by the very nature of the word and the very model of Jesus, who gave his life as a ransom for many.

# Chapter 5 endnotes

[1] Castillo, Metosalema. *The Church in Thy House* (Alliance Publishers, 1982), p 9.

[2] Ibid.

[3] 1 Corinthians 12:18, Ephesians 4:7, and 1 Corinthians 12:11.

[4] Filson, Floyd F. *Journal of Biblical Literature* (unknown, 1939), pp 110-112.

[5] Brown, *Theological Dictionary of New Testament Theology*, Volume 3 (Grand Rapids, MI: Eerdmans, 1971), pp 349-350.

[6] Bruce, F.F. *The Epistle to the Ephesians* (Toronto: Fleming H. Revell Company, 1961), p 86.

[7] Schwarz, Christian. *Color Your World with Natural Church Development*, p 106.

[8] Watson, David. *I Believe in the Church*, p 254.

[9] Niebuhr, Richard. *The Social Sources of Denominations* (Kessenger Publishers, 1984), p 24.

[10] One helpful resource is *Biblical Eldership, an Urgent Call to Restore Biblical Church Leadership* by Alexander Strauch (Lewis & Roth, 1995)

# CHAPTER SIX

## Leadership Re-Engineered: Stewarding Our Lives

Almighty God; We make our earnest prayer that Thou wilt keep the United States in Thy holy protection; that Thou wilt incline the hearts of the citizens to cultivate a spirit of subordination and obedience to government; and entertain a brotherly affection and love for one another and for their fellow citizens of the United States at large. And finally that Thou wilt most graciously be pleased to dispose us all to do justice, to love mercy, and to demean ourselves with that charity, humility, and pacific temper of mind which were the characteristics of the Divine Author of our blessed religion, and without a humble imitation of whose example in these things we can never hope to be a happy nation. Grant our supplication, we beseech Thee, through Jesus Christ our Lord. Amen.

George Washington, his prayer for the nation, on a plaque inside the Washington Monument, Washington, D.C.

*By this all men shall know that you are my disciples — by the way you love each other.*
John 13:35

*Each one should use whatever gift he or she has received to serve others, as good stewards of the grace of God in its various forms. If anyone speaks, speak as if speaking the very words of God. If anyone serves, serve with the strength that God provides, so that in all things God may be praised through Jesus Christ. To Him be the glory and the power for ever and ever.*
1 Peter 4:10-11

**You have to live the life you were born to live.**
Mother Superior to Maria in *The Sound of Music*

What happens when the patterns of the world influence the daily life of the Christian? As we discussed in Section I, the influences of the leadership myth, individualism, and the ladder mentality are real and have ongoing, profound impact on how Christians and Christian leaders live out their daily lives.

> **"I no longer assume that Christians will act Christianly."**

After ten years of doing team-building seminars, interspersed with my overseas trips to other cultures, I found myself beginning such events with the following statement to Christian leaders and their teams: "I no longer assume that Christians will act Christianly." I could see the impact of narcissism, entitlement, dissatisfaction, and sarcasm affecting relational dynamics on every ministry team with which I worked.

Bruce Malina writes on American individualism:

In our culture [U.S.A.], we are brought up to stand on our own two feet, as distinctive wholes, distinctive individuals, male and female. We are motivated to behave in the "right" way, alone, regardless of what others might say. In our process of identity formation, we tend to believe and act as though we do so singly and alone, since each person is a unique sphere of feeling and knowing, of judging and acting.... This is individualism, and this sort of individualism is rare in the world's cultures today. It was totally absent from the New Testament.[1]

While individualism was almost nonexistent in the New Testament era, it is the dominant pattern of the day in the United States. Because of this, we can no longer assume that Christian leaders will necessarily act like the stewards of their relationships and of theirs and others' powerful gifts. We cannot presume this, even though, for many postmodernists, "individualism is giving way to a longing to belong."[2] Just because Christian leaders are called to be good stewards of their gifts and their relationships does not mean that they (1) will act as good stewards or even (2) know how to act as good stewards.

Given that reality, let us more deeply examine each of our two stewardship areas.

## Tenaciously Pursuing Healthy Relationships

Since God's strategies are primarily relational, and since broken relationships dot the landscape of every city and county in the U.S., learning to be a good steward of healthy relationships is not optional for the Christian leader. With the imperative to speak the truth in love as we grow up together in Christ, the unity and maturity of relationships is essential — and must be priorities in the good steward's daily life.

Is it any wonder that the qualifications for one to function in spiritual authority are mostly relational standards? Note Titus 1:6: "An elder must be blameless, the husband of but one wife ... whose children believe and are not open to the charge of being wild and disobedient." Titus then says that, if an overseer is to be a steward, one entrusted with God's work, then that person must have a righteous lifestyle, which he describes in 1:7-8. To have the privilege and responsibility of providing spiritual authority, one must live right relationally.

Paul, in 1 Timothy 3:1-10, includes the ability to manage his own family well in a list of requirements for overseers and deacons: "If anyone does not know how to manage his own family, how can he take care of God's church?"[3] The vast majority

> **The model of right relationship appears to be much more important than the capacity to lead large groups or preach with great illustrations.**

of qualities listed in this passage have to do with relational qualities. The ability to teach — to rightly divide the word of truth — is the only real "serving competency" requirement listed here. The model of right relationship appears to be much more important than the capacity to lead large groups or preach with great illustrations.

Here is how one leader, Steven Gilbert, reacts to this new insight about spiritual leadership qualifications: "of all the qualifications listed in Timothy and Titus — there are around twenty-three — only one and maybe two have to do with a skill. I think that shows us some things: (1) God puts a lot more stock in the character modeled in the context of relationships than in skill: (2) People who have strong character in relationships are more qualified than brilliant, skilled people in the household of God! (3) We are emphasizing training in the wrong areas, that is, skill-set-focused training rather than relational stewardship training.[4]

Sometimes I do wish the priority for the leader were productivity and impressiveness, or strong conversion numbers and leading a big or growing ministry. For many that is always the standard. But no Scripture passages refer to such requirements for leaders. "Growing a big church" and "capacity to lead and manage a lot of people" are not on any of the lists. The character and intent to manage right, healthy relationships is the biblical model in organic body life. The good steward of relationships models a Christian lifestyle and, as we see again in section III, is also a good steward of his or her gifts and of those gifts in others serving alongside.

In college I was part of a ministry called seekers. My first serious role of responsibility was to take charge of the weekly program for our fellowship meeting. Because of my gift of exhortation I wanted very much to get to know and encourage each member of our program team, even though I did not yet understand my own gifting. It seemed to me that a cheerful team would be better suited to provide thoughtful and creative programs.

What I did not realize was that I was meeting the first essential biblical criterion for being a steward — a good manager of the relationships entrusted to me. We had fun and developed real friendships all around. One of the results was a wonderful year of programming, where we saw many lives changed and people moving out as a result to reach their friends for Christ.

**Cultivate Healthy Attitudes in Your Relationships with Others.** It always starts with our heart attitudes, how we approach any situation or relationship. In Philippians, Paul gives a very concise exhortation about our attitudes in the stewardship of right relationships, including the identification of our primary role model in relationships:

> If you have any encouragement from being united with Christ,
> if any comfort from his love,
> if any fellowship with the Spirit,
> if any tenderness and compassion,
> then make my joy complete by being like-minded,
> having the same love,
> being one in spirit and purpose.
> Do nothing out of selfish ambition or vain conceit,
> but in humility consider others better than yourself.
> Each of you should look not only to your own interests,
> but also to the interests of others.

> Your attitude should be the same as that of Christ Jesus:
> Who, being in very nature God,
> did not consider equality with God something to be grasped,

but made himself nothing,
taking the very nature of a servant,
being made in human likeness.
And being found in appearance as a man,
he humbled himself and became obedient to death —
even death on a cross. (Philippians 2: 1-8)

Paul reminds us of our third word from chapter 5, *minister* (or *servant*), as key in the heart attitudes of the Christian and the Christian leader. And who better to portray the nature of servanthood than Jesus. The cost of unity is great — which is most certainly why Jesus is our role model for such. To consider others as more important than yourself or to do nothing out of selfish ambition — these are actions that we can consistently take only with the model of Jesus before us and the power of his Spirit guiding us. Paul says, "It simply cannot always be about you!" And Jesus reveals the essence of that truth to us on the cross.

Concentrate Your Actions in Right Relationships. Let us move from baseline attitudes that shape our actions to the actions themselves. Paul again supplies some helpful standards, this time in Ephesians 4:

*Therefore each of you must put off falsehood and speak truthfully to his neighbor, for we are all members of one body. "In your anger do not sin"; do not let the sun go down while you are still angry, and do not give the devil a foothold. ...*

*Do not let any unwholesome talk come out of your mouths [no sarcasm!], but only what is helpful for building others up according to their needs, that it may be a benefit for those who listen. ... Get rid of all bitterness, rage and anger, brawling and slander, along with every form of malice. Be kind and compassionate to one another, forgiving each other, just as in Christ God forgave you. (Ephesians 4: 25-27, 29, 31-32)*

Note that these words follow the concepts from Ephesians highlighted in chapters 4 and 5 in this book:

- the body of Christ as the fullness of God

- the building up of God's household into a place where he lives by his Spirit

- the economy of his grace

Ephesians 4-6 extensively discuss how to live out right relationships as believers. First Paul tells us what we really are as believers and then he illuminates how we are to live with one another. This profoundly reaffirms that the primary way people know that we are Christians is indeed by the way we live out our relationships in love, as Jesus stated so plainly in John 13:34-35.

Is there any wonder why those who are in positions of leadership are to be intentional stewards of right, healthy, growing, submitted relationships? Please reread George Washington's prayer in the chapter introduction. Notice his emphasis on right relationships. Right relationships breed a healthy community where Christians can live and work together for the common good.

In our changing postmodern world, authenticity is of especially great importance. Brett Yon writes: "Authenticity is more highly valued than smooth appearances. The nicely packaged approaches to everything from advertising to zoology do not move them [post-modernist] ... *Real* is what they value over being right."[5] Authenticity speaks to the heart of real community, and to the stewardship responsibility of the leader in both modeling and encouraging healthy relationships.

**Live Out Reconciled, Renewed Relationships.** Healthy relationships demand right, reconciled relationships. Mending broken relationships is key to the whole fabric of the body of Christ and central in our witness to a lost world. It is of strategic importance that the different parts of the body be built up and built together, with great sensitivity to mending torn fabric, that is, broken relationships. Thus, an important role of the steward and the equipper is to take great care in modeling and encouraging reconciliation in relationships. That is, the good steward seeks to stay healthy in relationships, seeking to be at peace with all people. In Matthew 5:9, Jesus blessed peacemakers and called them sons and daughters of God! Scripture is clear: reconciliation truly is important!

> Mending broken relationships is key to the whole fabric of the body of Christ and central in our witness to a lost world.

Take note of Ephesians 6: 10-18. The first thing that follows more than two chapters of "how to live right relationships" is how to stand firm amidst spiritual warfare — to withstand the fiery darts from the evil one. Perhaps there is a reason for the location of this spiritual warfare passage. Indeed! If the concept of spiritual warfare is real, would it not follow that Satan is seeking to create havoc in Christian relationships?

Would he not, for example, seek to encourage an overseer to break fellowship with his spouse or co-workers or friends, in order to create more and more disunity and discord wherever possible?

What better way to break apart the body of Christ that is God's household than to tear the fabric through unreconciled or broken relationships? And what of leaders who have not learned, or do not understand how, to live in right relationships — or to reconcile when one has been torn apart?

Through my team-building work with churches and mission teams all over the world, I have observed in many different settings how American Christians live out their relationships with one another. Presently, there is an epidemic running rampant in the hundreds of settings in which I have worked in the West: the disease of broken relationships. And this ailment is wreaking havoc not just in the secular arena but also among Christians. Now, given our present context and discussion, it all makes sense as to why this would be true. Steve Weldon says it this way: "Culturally, we see all failure as personal failure rather than also impacting the entire body of Christ."[6]

My first realization about the depth of this issue occurred in the CoMission days of 1993-98 in the former Soviet Union. We discovered an intriguing yet devastating pattern in many of our 200 teams in 68 cities during those years. Often, if an American went to Russia or the Ukraine with a significant relationship left unresolved at home, it had dramatic impact on that person's team on the field. It was as if somehow the rift back home was carried into the fresh situation and created a new rift in the CoMission team. I do not understand exactly how this works in the spiritual arena, but we had scores of teams confirm this reality. Groups struggled dramatically or even imploded on the field in large part because of previously unresolved discord. A diseased body part can harm or even kill the whole body. Fellowship fabric that is torn will remain tattered and further fray without healing reconciliation.

Do you recall our early discussion of the ease with which some people throw off anything — and in some cases anyone — because they are not happy with it or with them? This is at the core of our world of broken relationships. Self-serving Christians will leave relationships and churches at the drop of a hat for any number of personal reasons. The result is weeping in heaven as the brokenness dominates.

As leaders, it is essential for us to practice the reconciliation of relationships in our lives and in the lives of our team members, group, or ministry. Consider the counsel given by Jesus about relational discord when someone else appears to have something against you:

> "Therefore, if you are offering your gift at the altar and there remember that your brother has something against you, leave your gift there in front of the altar. First go and be reconciled to your brother; then come and offer your gifts." (Matthew 5: 23-24)

Consider a situation where someone has actually committed a sin against you. Again, Jesus offers wise counsel:

> "If your brother sins against you, go and show him his fault, just between the two of you. If he listens to you, you have won your brother over. But if he will not listen, take one or two others along, so that 'every matter may be established by the testimony of two or three witnesses.' If he refuses to listen to them, tell it to the church; and if he refuses to listen even to the church, treat him as you would a pagan or a tax collector." (Matthew 18: 15-17)

What should we do about someone who has been caught in sinful behavior? Paul addresses that issue and emphasizes just how much we need each other as supporting ligaments when it comes to standing against sin in our own lives.

> Brothers, if someone is caught in a sin, you who are spiritual should restore him gently. But watch yourself, or you also may be tempted. Carry each other's burdens, and in this way you will fulfill the law of Christ. If anyone thinks he is something when he is nothing, he deceives himself. (Galatians 6: 1-3)

Finally, what about that general issue of sin in the lives of each of us? How do we stay reconciled in body life? The apostle James' counsel is clear:

> Therefore confess your sins to each other and pray for each other that you may be healed. ... My brothers, if one of you should wander from the truth and someone should bring him back, remember this: whoever turns a sinner from the error of his way will save him from death and cover over a multitude of sins. (James 5: 16, 19)

The body life implications of this last passage are tremendous. It means that all of us, leaders or otherwise, are to be open about our battles with sin, not only to help keep us on track individually, but also for unity and maturity in the whole body. It does matter to the whole group or church if even one person is unresolved in a relationship. It does matter if someone leaves a local church because of a rift but is not held accountable for failing to seek reconciliation. It does matter that repentance — turning from sin — takes place in a broken relationship where such is needed for healing or release.

> **It does matter to the whole group or church if even one person is unresolved in a relationship.**

For many leaders the need is very personal to come clean amidst their own battles with sin. This issue is very personal to me, for I watched my father struggle with this as a pastor in a local church. In my early twenties, I came home from college and was having a conversation with Dad. Suddenly, out of the clear blue, he shared that he was struggling personally.

He admitted to me that, in his thirty-five years of full-time ministry, he had never felt free to admit to any church members any struggles with sin or weakness in his life. He said that he had been trained to be the shepherd, the strong one who was to be a model for the struggling sheep. He also confessed that he was really afraid to admit that he battled at all with sin — how could he as a spiritual leader? But now he had realized his own deep need to come clean and find reconciliation in his own heart. That day, my father began to free himself from a lot of baggage. How about you, as a leader, a steward, an equipper?

We need much guidance as we work more actively and intentionally on the stewardship of our relationships in the body of Christ. Many people have found tremendous support from Ken Sande's books and his ministry, Peacemakers. He has a fifteen-year track record of helping many thousands of Christians in the practical realities of working through relational conflict and reconciliation.[7]

In my life, I address my own joys and battleground areas in my small group of men to whom I am accountable and in whom I find real safety to be honest about the challenges from within and from without. In any given week, one or two of the five of us bring up real issues for which we need encouragement or an accountable checkpoint. In fact, earlier on this very day that I write these words, I received an email from one of these friends checking up on an area of struggle I shared last week. And last week I spent four hours of email communication with a brother whom I mentor overseas. The purpose was to clear up a significant misunderstanding between us. I could have used those four hours in some other creative, strategic, programmatic way, but the stewardship of reconciling relationships took top priority. The managing of healthy relationships — that is reconciled friendships, work relationships, and marriages — is based on a high level of encouragement, safety, trust, and accountability. Often it takes plain old hard work at two-way communication!

Once upon a time Adam and Eve lived in an intimate relationship with God. However, they disobeyed him. The result? They both hid from God and experienced a break in relationship with him. We have been repeating similar patterns with similar results ever since.

Reconciling our relationships with God and with one another is an essential stewardship responsibility for every spiritual leader — for every Christian.

## Courageously Using Our Spiritual Gifts

The New Testament has revealed God's relational strategy as well as the importance of being an intentional steward of all relationships. Acts 2, 1 Peter 4, and Ephesians 4 bring out the importance of spiritual gifts ministry alongside relationships, and the involvement of the Trinity in creating community and dispensing gifts. Given this, what special guidelines can help stewards and equippers be more intentional in discovering and using their spiritual gifts? Three important concepts have revealed themselves to me over the past ten years that are expressly tied to organic body life and the stewardship of spiritual gifts:

**1. The process of sober estimation.** The first concept comes from Romans 12:3, the "ministry of sober estimation." It is the hidden principle between Romans 12:1-2 and 12:4-6.

> Therefore, I urge you, brothers and sisters, in view of God's mercy, to offer your bodies as living sacrifices, holy and pleasing to God — this is your spiritual act of worship. Do not conform any longer to the pattern of this world, but be transformed by the renewing of your mind. Then you will be able to test and approve what God's will is — his good, pleasing and perfect will. (12:1-2)

> For by the grace given me I say to every one of you: Do not think of yourself more highly than you ought, but rather think of yourself with sober judgment, in accordance with the

measure of faith God has given you. (12:3)

Just as each of us has one body with many members, and these members do not all have the same function, so in Christ we who are many form one body, and each member belongs to all the others. We have different gifts, according to the grace given us. If a man's gift is prophesying, let him use it in proportion to his faith. (12:4-6)

Many Christians have memorized Romans 12:1-2, as it is a significant passage about the initial steps for discerning the good and perfect will of God. Choosing to become a living sacrifice by seeking to be transformed in Christ, rather than being conformed to the world, is essential. In verse 3, Paul continues with very specific advice on the next steps for discerning the good and perfect will of God. That verse also introduces the body life and spiritual gifts passage in verses 4-6.

First, Paul says to not think more highly of yourself than you ought – in terminology  pertinent to our process: "Ladder climbing is not helpful and pride will not cut it!" Second, Paul suggests you make a sober estimate of yourself – that is, look deeply in self-examination at who you are – as a practical step in the process of discerning God's will.

My personal discovery of this remarkable principle came about in the late nineties as I was battling with the reality that thousands of Christian leaders do not have a clear sense of who they are in Christ, as described in chapter 1. For numerous reasons, many of us have never truly stopped to take stock of who we already are in Christ before we move ahead to the next project, plan, or activity. Peter Drypolcher, a missionary in Africa, said it best: "There is little or no introspection in leaders in general."[8] I have taken an informal survey on this issue for years in groups that I train by asking this question: "How many of you have spent at least two hours with another person talking only about who you are in Christ and what spiritual gifts you have?" Overall, less than ten percent of the people claimed to have spent 120 minutes of life making an intentional, sober estimate of who they are! Most of us simply do not stop to take stock of who we are giftwise and where we are relationally.

Paul continues with more practical counsel in 12: 4-6. If you want to see yourself clearly and with sober estimation, follow two principles: (1) See yourself in proper perspective as one among others in the body of Christ, not having the same function as others. God's creativity has caused you to be unique in the body. (2) Seek to understand what spiritual gifts you have. That is, make a sober estimate of what portion of grace you have received in God's economy of grace. Again we see that the pairing of body life relationships and spiritual gifts is a recurring theme that appears often throughout the New Testament.

So, for those of us wanting to discern the good and perfect will of God, we have clear counsel from the Apostle Paul: Don't build yourself up in inappropriate ways, but rather make a serious, clear-headed examination of who you are. First, realize that as one among so many others in the organic body of Christ, your function is likely different than that of others. Then seek to clearly identify what spiritual gifts you have been given to carry out your part in the body life functions.

Observe that Paul practiced what he preached, as he unmistakably identifies his spiritual gifts in 1 Timothy 2:7 and 2 Timothy 1:11 — evangelist, apostle, and teacher. Paul took his own counsel from Romans 12:3-6 and came to a clear self-perception of his distinctive body life role and his unique gift combination, so much so that he communicates it to Timothy and now to all of us.

In Roman's 15:15-20, as Paul talks about his ministry, he actually reveals two of those three gifts: evangelism and apostleship. As he talks about his kingdom work, his true identity powerfully rises to the surface! Note also that Paul reveals his ministry burden or passion as well in this passage. He is compelled to invest the whole of his life in the Gentiles, wherever that might take him. In Romans 15: 28, Paul acknowledges this could take him all the way to Spain.

I use the term *ministry identity* to refer to the combination of one's spiritual gifts and ministry burden or passion. (Note a simple overview of ministry identity in Appendix A.) This is not what you do for God, but rather what God has already supernaturally prepared in you to play your body life part. This is why I named my team-building assessment workbook *Discovering Your Ministry Identity*.[9] For reasons that should now be obvious, the best place for Christians to discover who they are in Christ is in the context of committed relationships. Christian Schwarz writes, "Empowering leaders can rejoice ... with all their heart because they know that God has a unique calling for every individual."[10]

Sober estimation and stewardship of your ministry identity fit hand in hand with freeing the leader from the battle of self-centered searching for significance through roles and special skills training. According to Howard Snyder:

**The identifying of spiritual gifts brings to the fore ... the issue**

of commitment. Doors will close on a million possibilities. Commitment at my point of gifts means that I must give up being a straddler. Somewhere deep inside I know this. Life will not be the smorgasbord I have made it, sampling and tasting here and there.[11]

**2. The 65-35 Principle.** From this, in fact, I have developed a simple way for people to think soberly about how to be stewards of God's grace in their lives. I call it the "65-35 Principle," our second gifts stewardship guideline. Thousands of Christian leaders have found this principle to be very helpful for practically living out the stewardship of who they are in Christ.

First, to effectively steward your gifts, seek to spend at least 65 percent of your time in your areas of gifting and burden or passion. Since God desires intentional stewardship of who he has designed us to be, would it not follow suit to seek to live out who he designed you to be on a regular, intentional basis? The "65" represents the intent to spend at least 65 percent of your time using your gifts, that is, significantly more than half of your time.

In a perfect world, it would be wonderful to serve God with all my gifts all the time. However that has proven to not be realistic in body life ministry where close to 80 percent of the players do not know what their parts are or do not know how to play their parts or are simply unwilling to do so. Some people, after learning this principle, call it the "75-25" or "80-20 principle," believing that Christians should spend even more time being who they are in Christ. It does not matter which numbers you use, as long as you train and release people to focus the majority of their time on their soberly estimated gifts.

The "35" represents the time spent in roles that do not utilize our gifts. Each of us will often need to fill roles that do not relate to who we are and may not utilize the power of the Spirit. The key is to spend only up to 35 percent of our time in that and no more.

Therein lies the battleground. The key to stewardship is learning how to spend significantly more than half your time focusing on your gifts. Far and away the biggest problem I have observed for Christian leaders is that they end up spending 70 percent of their time in the 35 category, with the resultant loss of spiritual power and fruits of the Spirit. That is, they spend the broad majority of their time in areas where God did not design nor empower them! And, given that the root word of spiritual gift is the word *char*, or joy,[12] there is a tremendous loss of joy in serving. Not experiencing any joy in your ministry or serving? There is a good chance that you are not being a good steward of the gifts through which the Holy Spirit has empowered you.

Many Christians do find freedom and focus in learning to be who they are in Christ! And, for many of those, a key is that they stop trying to be someone who they are not. Then *no* becomes a spiritual word. When this happens, equipping and releasing these Christians to play their parts becomes a lot easier. Equippers find freedom in being themselves — and free others to the same reality by getting out of their way.

> **Stop trying to be someone who you are not.**

**3. The power in spiritual gifts.** A third organic principle has come to the fore as I watch and understand more about body life ministry and the stewardship of spiritual gifts. I learned it in central Asia and Kazakhstan.

The very first opportunity I had to work with Kazakhs six years ago, I came across an unusual problem. As I talked about spiritual gifts and how critical it is that leaders understand who they are in Christ from a body life standpoint, I discovered that Kazakhs have no word that translates as "supernatural." So, in my teaching about spiritual gifts, I had to think of a different, creative way to talk about the nature of spiritual gifts. With hand motions moving up from my waist and outward, I communicated that spiritual gifts are where God powerfully works through you. The Kazakhs were visibly moved and, frankly, so was I.

At that moment I realized something. Spiritual gifts really are the power of God, more than just natural talents or learned skills. It is where the power of God rises up beyond the natural and into the supernatural, powerful realm. I had known this in my head, but at that moment it became heart knowledge. From that time on the Holy Spirit began to affect almost everyone whom I have trained since.

Shortly after this personal "aha" moment shared with the Kazakhs, I began to notice that there were clear New Testament references to power as it related to spiritual gifts:

> I became a servant of this gospel by the gift of God's grace given me through the working of his power. (Ephesians 3: 7)

> We proclaim him, admonishing and teaching everyone with all wisdom, so that we may present everyone perfect in Christ. To this end I labor, struggling with all his energy which so

powerfully works in me. (Colossians 1: 28-29)

We have this treasure in jars of clay to show that this all-surpassing power is from God and not from us. (2 Corinthians 4: 7)

Spiritual gifts are not simply those activities in which we do well. Spiritual gifts are where God powerfully shows up in our actions by the power of the Holy Spirit. It is God at work, not something we can train or develop. For example, over the past twenty years I have been amazed at how few school teachers have the spiritual gift of teaching, that is, the supernatural capacity to teach God's Word in such a way that people understand. Spiritual gifts are given, not trained; gifts are a manifestation of the Spirit's power, not a culmination of years of learning! "No amount of theological training or human pressure can bestow *charisma* [spiritual gifts] on a person."[13]

I have shared this new insight in every training situation since that day, and the response of others has been truly amazing. People began to grasp the real, practical difference between natural, God-given talents and skills that we have from birth and the supernatural spiritual gifts, which we receive by grace at conversion and the infilling presence of the Holy Spirit.

**Equipping Gifts and Supporting Gifts.** From the power language and this new dynamic understanding of gifting has come another of the most important insights God has given me to share with Christians and especially leaders over the past fifteen years. As you make a sober estimate of who you are in Christ and seek to live out the 65-35 principle, how will you understand the powerful function of the gifts given to you? Peter and Paul give us invaluable functional language to illuminate this matter.

Consider words from Peter in the already familiar passage in 1 Peter 4:10-11. Verse 10 brings us back to the stewardship of God's grace by using our gifts: "Each one should use whatever gifts he [or she] has received to serve others, as good stewards of God's grace in its many forms". Now note verse 11:

If anyone speaks he [or she] should do it as one speaking the very words of God. If anyone serves he [or she] should do it with the strength God provides, so that in all things God may be praised through Jesus Christ. To him be the glory and the power forever and ever. Amen.

I have labored over the past twenty years to understand and work with spiritual gifts from a functional standpoint, that is, how do gifts work when you use them? Two words come to the fore from Ephesians 4:11-16 that, combined with 1 Peter 4, give us a simple but profound means to help others grasp the functional nature of their powerful spiritual gifts. The first word is one of our major words from the last chapter — *equipping.* Clearly there are gifts whose primary purpose is to equip, mend, protect, and prepare the saints for the work of ministry. All the gifts that seem to fit in the equipping category are gifts where God's power is revealed in words — the words of the person using the gift:

- Evangelism

- exhortation

- Faith

- Knowledge/word of knowledge

- Leadership

- Pastoring

- Prophecy

- Wisdom/word of wisdom

NOTE: Some would include discernment of spirits, tongues and interpretation of tongues, healing, intercession, and miracles. I put these in a separate category called "gifts growing out of prayer and worship."[14]

Equipping gifts portray God's power in the words spoken, as noted in 1 Peter 4:11 - "*...as if speaking the very words of God.*" The purpose of these gifts is to powerfully train and release saints to their God-designed parts through words spoken in the power of the Holy Spirit.

The second word is *supporting,* from the "supporting ligament" phrase in Ephesians 4:16. Some gifts' primary purpose is to support and serve. In these gifts, the power is in the actions, as Peter suggests. God works powerfully through the serving actions; that is, the power is not in the words but in the actions. Have you ever heard someone say, "I don't need to talk; my actions will speak for themselves"? Usually that person has strong supporting gifts! Here are the gifts I would include in this functional category:

- Giving

- Helps

- Service

- Mercy

- Administration

Thus, our functional approach portrays spiritual gifts as powerful in words (equipping) or actions (supporting). (For more information on this functional approach to gifts, see my assessment workbooks for individuals and teams.)[15]  But do not miss Peter's key point in 4:11: Whether our gifts

> **If we minister in his power, as the verse says, there will be no question about who gets the glory!**

are equipping gifts with super-charged words or supporting gifts with super-charged actions, they are to be shared in the strength and power of God. Why? The reason is simple: If we minister in his power, as the verse says, there will be no question about who gets the glory! No one gets to climb the ladder of glory or significance because of our gifts. We serve in his power so that all the glory and praise go to him alone.

After we discern our spiritual gifts, each of us will fit one of the following three categories: a person's spiritual gifts can be only supporting gifts, only equipping gifts, or a combination of equipping and supporting gifts. This functional understanding will provide practical guidance for many, as has already been proven true in my work on five continents.

Of all the insights God has given me, two have proven to have the greatest impact over my past twenty years of training Christian leaders. First was the insight shared in chapter 1 about people whose only spiritual gifts are supporting gifts. Such gifted players, by God's design, are not able to lead powerfully. Providentially, many of these Christians have found the freedom to use their supporting gifts and not feel any pressure to move into a leadership or equipping role. Since there is no ladder to climb, Christians with only supporting gifts have no pressure to try to be something they are not. The joy comes in powerful serving and supporting, not in any effort to move up or try to become more important by the world's standards for success.

The second insight is for those who have a combination of equipping and supporting gifts. Equipping gifts are designed to equip and release others to play their gifted parts. Supporting gifts, on the other hand, are designed to serve or support others with powerful actions. By God's design, such gifted folk would rather themselves do the serving than release others to do so! That is, God engineered people with supporting gifts to find joy in helping through their own actions — not in equipping and releasing others. So, when a person with a combination of equipping and supporting gifts and is in a leading or equipping role, an unusual tendency is intrinsically found. They will, due to their own gift combination, have a hard time releasing certain ministry functions to others. Because of their gifts, a part of who they are wants to equip and release, but the supporting gift part would rather "do it myself."

I have seen this confirmed by hundreds of people in scores of different ministry settings, and in at least ten other cultures. Such leaders with this combination of gifting realize that they will have to be much more intentional about releasing support functions to others when they are in an equipping role. They cannot hold on to doing things themselves, as they will greatly limit body life ministry by not sharing ministry functions with others. People whose equipping-supporting gift combination includes the supporting gift of administration have to be particularly careful on this point. Holding tightly onto serving functions can become a huge control issue for such a person.

Our spiritual gifts are so important that God calls us to be good stewards of these powerful grace gifts. They define how the power of God is released in our lives of spiritual service. Please make a sober estimate so that you can continue to grow as an intentional steward of who you already are in Christ.

**The Power of the Spirit Changes Personality!** The revelation of this truth has so intrigued me from that day in Kazakhstan that, over the past ten years, I have developed a way to observe the differences between natural talents and supernatural spiritual gifts. Since 1995 I have worked with a tool called *The Birkman Method*, a highly sophisticated personality profiling tool used primarily in the corporate world.[16] It is an extremely accurate gauge of a person's personality and natural talents from eleven different angles. From the start, I have used this exhaustive resource alongside my spiritual gifts workbooks, particularly *Discovering Your Ministry Identity* and *Your Leadership Grip*. I used the following diagram to clarify the different purposes of the two assessment sets (see figure 6-a):

# The Power of Your Spiritual Gifts

## Energized Through and Beyond Your Personality

**The Spiritual Gifts Triangle**
Three Angles on How You Are Powerful

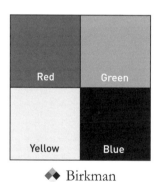

**The Lifestyle Grid**
Your Baseline Personality

Figure 6-a

In 1999 I began to realize there might be a way to separate natural talents and spiritual gifts from these two assessment sets. I had *The Birkman Method*, with a forty year track record of precision insights, and my workbooks, with a ten-year track record of helping leaders and team members to more accurately discern their spiritual gifting. Then God gave me the Kazakh power insight in 2000, and I became motivated at a new level!

I began to intently watch the differences between people's Birkman personality results and their spiritual gifts. The first major observation was that many Christian leaders whose natural style was more nondirective or introverted had spiritual gifts that were verbally powerful. This did not make sense, unless the powerful working of the Spirit in spiritual gifts actually changed a person's natural personality. That is, the Spirit-empowered equipping gifts caused a verbal power to surface in people who were naturally nondirective in their personality work style. I offered this interpretation to every person I encountered who had this combination, scores of people, and they were ecstatic! Finally they understood that, to a person, they were powerfully direct in style with their gifts but in their natural personality were more introverted. They were especially pleased to finally understand this, because it had been a source of serious internal conflict.

In 2003 I approached both Birkman and ChurchSmart, my publisher, about the possibility of developing a resource that would formally wed these gifts and a personality assessing processes. The result of that interaction is called the *Grip/Birkman Blueprint*.[17] Combining *Your Leadership Grip*, my assessment workbook that assesses spiritual gifts from three different angles with three different sets of words, with *The Birkman Method's* assessment of personality and talents, has given me an ongoing laboratory to continue observing the differences between natural talents and spiritual gifting. Stated plainly, the Holy Spirit powerfully affects one's personality according to the specific gifts given a person. The movement can be in any direction from a person's usual personality style. We call this movement the "Dotted Diamond."[18] Our team of Grip/Birkman Blueprint trainers and coaches is excited about what we are learning and will learn about the impact of Spirit-empowered spiritual gifts on a person's natural behavior. It truly is the power of God!

## Conclusion

Jesus was very clear in John 13:34-35. The mark of a Christian is the way he or she loves others. Our call to cultivate relationships through our attitudes and actions continues as a strategic priority from Acts 2 and 4 and into the writings of Paul and Peter.

Jesus also calls us to the stewardship of who we are, beginning with the parable of the talents in Matthew 25:14-30. He calls us to faithfully use that which has been given to us, no matter what we have been given. His call is clear. Paul and Peter lead us in clear steps toward becoming good stewards of who we are: first, through soberly estimating who we are, and then in seeking to be faithful stewards of God's grace in its many forms.

When we function in the power of his Spirit, not only does the dynamic work of the Spirit take over, but God also receives all the glory! Praise be to God

## Chapter 6 endnotes

[1] Malina, Bruce. *The New Testament World: Insights from Cultural Anthropology* (Louisville: John Knox Press, 1993), pp 54-55.

[2] Yon, Brett. "Taking the Next Step" (strategy paper prepared for a campus group in Lincoln, NE), p 2.

[3] 1 Timothy 3:5.

[4] Gilbert, Steven. Editorial notes offered in response to reading this book.

[5] Yon, p 2.

[6] Add Weldon quote...

[7] Ken Sande's resources can be found at *www.peacemaker.net.*

[8] Drypolcher, Peter. Notes prepared as a reader for this book.

[9] Ford, Paul R. *Discovering Your Ministry Identity* (ChurchSmart Resources, 1999). All of Paul's resources are available through *www.churchsmart.org.*

[10] Schwarz, Christian A. *Color Your World with Natural Church Development* (St. Charles, IL: ChurchSmart Resources), p 106.

[11] Snyder, Howard A. *The Problem with Wineskins* (Downers Grove, IL: Intervarsity Press, 1975), p 137.

[12] Brown,

[13] Watson, David, *I Believe in the Church* (Grand Rapids, MI: Eerdmans, 1978), p 264.

[14] These different gift categories can be found in Dr. Ford's *Unleash Your Church!, Getting Your Gifts in Gear, Discovering Your Ministry Identity,* and *Your Leadership Grip*, all available through *Churchsmart.com*

[15] Ibid.

[16] *www.birkman.com*

[17] An article giving more detail on the background and development of the *Grip/ Birkman Blueprint* can be found at *www.drpaulford.org/birkman_blueprint.htm* The resource is available through ChurchSmart Resources: 800-253-4276.

[18] The "Dotted Diamond" is the shift in one's Usual Style on the Birkman Lifestyle Grid (one's "diamond") to a probable new location. It reveals how one's spiritual gifts can change the nature of one's behavior in the power of the Spirit. The "dotted diamond" is the key linkage between the Birkman Lifestyle Grid and *Your Leadership Grip's* "Spiritual Gift Triangle," the depiction of one's natural personality and one's supernatural gifting for ministry.

# SECTION III

## Brand New Wineskins

As the old civic order gives way, Americans will have to craft a new one.... If all goes well there could be a renaissance of civic trust and more. Today's Third Turning problem — that Rubik's cube of crime, race, money, family, culture and ethics — will snap into a Fourth Turning solution. America's post-crisis answers will be as organically connected as today's questions seem hopelessly tangled.

William Strauss and Neil Howe
*The Fourth Turning*[1]

In the pragmatic view of the church, the church as the body of Christ has been replaced by an efficient corporation. The pastor is CEO and everyone else functions under the pastor's strong leadership. A meaningful and effective ministry is developed using marketing techniques and corporate organizational structures instead of attempting to recover the theological reality of the church.

Robert Webber
*Ancient-Future Faith*[2]

*See, I am doing a new thing!*
*Now it springs up; do you not perceive it?*
*I am making a way in the desert*
*And streams in the wasteland.*
Isaiah 42:9

*The Fourth Turning* is a fascinating sociological study claiming there is a four-cycle pattern that history has repeated over the twenty generations of American life. According to authors Strauss and Howe, the common "Third Turning," a cultural unraveling, has been very much in process over the past twenty years in the United States. What had been a national consensus in the early eighties is now becoming a broken mess, with individualism and competing values in almost every sector of society, including politics, ethics, and religion. Pessimism and blame are common reactions among the masses in regard to so many different issues. "the public reflects darkly on growing violence and incivility, widening inequality, pervasive distrust of institutions and leaders, and a debased popular culture."[3] What this sets up, say the authors, is the Fourth Turning, a season of extreme crisis that leads to new solutions and then, eventually, to a new period of spiritual awakening.

What is my point? We may very well be in the thick of a crisis in American Christian history. I believe this to be true, and in fact you have already read my earnest concerns in Section I. Robert Webber's words from *Ancient-Future Faith* describe the corporate approach to building local church body life that has become common today — and problematic. In our desire to help God enlarge his church, we have focused on the tasks of ministry, tied this to cultural ladder-climbing, and lost sight of the *who* in the body of Christ while we chase down the *how* (position, position, position!) and the *where* (location, location, location!). The organization has overtaken the organism, and consequently, the living body of Christ has had some unexpected constraints placed upon it.

Thankfully, the Christian community does not have to remain in the crisis or just weather the storm until things improve. In fact, like Martin Luther in the period of the Reformation, we can participate in a renaissance of new wineskins through organic body life. With his 95 theses posted on the door of a church in Wittenberg, Germany, Luther was responding to, among other issues, the sinful practice of purchasing "indulgences" as cheap grace. We can develop new language and new wineskins — and we do below — for Christian leaders who reject the ladder mentality so completely that we can begin to transform our Christian culture into one of interdependence![4] In fact, take note of Strauss and Howe's section opener: "America's post-crisis answers will be as organically connected as today's questions seem hopelessly tangled." How right they are, as understanding and applying the relational connectness of who we are in Christ provides helpful guidance for us. But that is for you to determine.

If God really is the one who lives and moves and desires to have his way among us, and calls us to be stewards of who we are and how he is moving among us, we have some changes to make. Chapter 7 addresses changes that are needed in our overall approach to Christian community and body life, as well as new wineskins that reveal God's heart for this challenging season. Chapter 8 addresses strategic leadership questions and how we can organically lead like Jesus and re-appropriate models that fit with New Testament language identified in chapter 5. Finally, chapter 9 applies our new wineskins in two key body life areas: vision and evangelism.

Consider Franklin Roosevelt's words as our challenge in this New Organic Reformation: "there is a mysterious cycle in human events. To some generations much is given. Of other generations much is expected. This generation has a mysterious rendezvous with destiny."[5]

# CHAPTER SEVEN

## Organic and Healthy Body Life

I believe that we have only just begun the process of discovering and inventing the new organizational forms that will inhabit the twenty-first century. To be responsible inventors and discoverers, we need the courage to let go of the old world, to relinquish most of what we have cherished, to abandon our interpretations about what does and doesn't work.

Margaret J. Wheatley
*Leadership and the New Science*[6]

He asked me, "Son of man, can these bones live?"
    I said, "O Sovereign Lord, you alone know."
This is what the Sovereign Lord says to these bones:
I will make breath enter you, and you will come to life.
I will attach tendons to you and make flesh come upon you
    and cover you with skin;
I will put my breath in you and you will come to life.
Then you will know that I am Lord.

Ezekiel 37:3, 5-7

Christian author Donald Miller says that we live in a time in history where we will be finding God in odd places.[7] The Lord of the Universe appears ready and willing to reveal his purposes to us through surprising sources. His desire to bring our dry bones to life with a fresh breath from his Spirit comes to us from many places, as the following unexpected source demonstrates.

Our present age represents an amazing time of discovery. The nature of life and the cosmos are revealing themselves to be one big splash of interconnections — a web of intertwined, overlapping systems that have become a part of today's postmodern consciousness.[8] Margaret Wheatley's intriguing book, *Leadership and the New Science*, reveals the momentous changes taking place in how scientists and engineers understand the functioning of the universe. Driving this, says Wheatley, have been discoveries in many fields of science and learning: biology, quantum physics, chaos theory, and self-organizing systems, to name a few. It turns out that the world is organically tied together at every level imaginable. Should Christians be shocked to discover that the natural web of relationships is more than just the organic, relational backbone of the body of Christ?

What is Wheatley's diagnosis amidst these new discoveries? Relationships — not individuals — are the basic organizing units of life. And, because of this, participation and cooperation are essential to survival in this interconnected world. Her concern is that we learn to work well together in these chaotic times, to move with grace and certainty in the midst of the organizations and communities in which we live.[9]

> **Relationships — not individuals — are the basic organizing units of life.**

Incidentally, Margaret Wheatley is not a scientist but rather a management consultant who studies organizational behavior. Her groundbreaking work, in its second edition, reveals some important insights about our discussion at hand. How shall we approach issues of leadership, vision, and organization in the body of Christ, this organic fellowship of the Holy Spirit on earth? Wheatley's insights help us to understand the nature of the new wineskins before us. Apparently, the world has always been organically intertwined. It is time for Christians to join in this discovery and recapture the biblical essence of organic body life in God's household!

With these new and revolutionary scientific discoveries of the cosmos' interconnectedness — which should be no surprise to Christians — has come a new world of possibilities that were not previously conceived. Note the last sentence from Wheatley's chapter opener: "To be responsible inventors and discoverers, we need the courage to let go of the old world, to relinquish most of what we have cherished, to abandon our interpretations about what does and doesn't work."

Take the current ordeal of skyrocketing fuel prices and the finite supply of nonrenewable energy shortages. No longer can we simply avoid the issue of other sources for energy. Where, in this natural world, might there be alternatives? Not surprisingly, entrepreneurial engineers and inventors are developing more sophisticated wind-powered generators and solar cells, and adding such sources as hydro-kinetic energy (i.e., underwater turbines) and wave power technology.[10] All of these sources are part of the natural web of life: wind, water, and light! There really are organic solutions to the issues we are facing — in the world *and* in the church.

Christians, we are in a season when we may have to let go of present understanding and move toward the new things that God has prepared for us. Consider Jesus' challenge that echoes the words we just read:

> "No one tears a patch from a new garment and sews it on an old one. If he does, he will have torn the new garment, and the patch from the new will not match the old. And no one pours new wine into old wineskins. If he does, the new wine will burst the skins, the wine will run out and the wineskins will be ruined. No, new wine must be poured into new wineskins." (Luke 5: 36-38)

**Why New Wineskins?** Let's face it. There is truth to the issues presented in Section I: the church cannot be a collection of individual free agents, feeling entitled and dissatisfied, each seeking after his or her own fulfillment. The church and its multi-level training models should not encourage its spiritual leaders to climb the leadership ladder at will, searching for bigger and better roles for greater personal significance. Nor can it continue to live out sarcasm as an art form or blindly allow Christians to move around the body of Christ at-large with unreconciled relationships.

There is truth to Robert Webber's earlier words: "In the pragmatic view of the church, the church as the body of Christ has been replaced by an efficient corporation."[11] Putting on the world's wineskins, or at least mixing and matching the world's systems and the Spirit, is not working. We look too much the same and we currently seem to be powerless to change the world. We simply cannot reach the world as the living body of Christ with current Christian organizational models.

As Roland Allen so aptly stated, "Even if the supply of men and funds from Western sources were unlimited and we could cover the whole globe with an army of millions of foreign missionaries and establish stations thickly all over the world, the method would rapidly reveal its weakness."[12] Our leader-driven and vision-driven organizational models are simply not the way that God intended for the body to be built up and the world to be reached. The strength is not in the structures, the financial resources, or the one right strategy that we determine. The wisdom and power flow primarily through our relationship with Christ and our organic or natural interconnectedness within the body — relationships!

How do we access that which God has prepared for us? What does it mean to be organic, to be God's earthly community, to be in the world but not of it?

## New Wineskins: Organic Sizes and Shapes

Margaret Wheatley writes, "The organization of a living system bears no resemblance to organizational charts. Life is made up of relationships and uses networks. We still rely on boxes. But even as we draw our boxes, people are ignoring them and organizing as life does, through networks of relationships."[13] So it is with the body of Christ.

Here is a crystallized definition of organic: "Organic equals relational." Further, an organism is an interconnected, interdependent web of living cells that is life giving among its members but also able to easily multiply new cells. God's strategy is all about relationships, organically imbedded in our new wineskins, and of course modeled by Jesus and his disciples two thousand years ago. You might say that our "new" wineskins are "old-new" wineskins. We intend here to recapture those wineskins — those applications —that Jesus modeled. What is the new wineskin about which Jesus spoke? It is the container that holds the new wine, usually made from sheep or goatskin. We identify below eight new skins that will effectively hold the new wine God has for us in this season of life. (Chapter 7 addresses wineskins 1 through 4, chapter 8 describes wineskins 5 and 6, and chapter 9 explains wineskins 7 through 9.)

**Wineskin #1: The Stewardship of Relationships and Spiritual Gifts.** Over the thirty years in which I have been involved in various Christian ministries, I have experienced only two areas where spiritual multiplication took place spontaneously. I recently came to realize that these two areas are (a) the same two stewardship topics discussed in chapter 6, and (b) the only two areas where all three persons of the Trinity are said to actively participate! The following two examples are practical applications of this first wineskin.

The first example is primarily a model of *the stewardship of right relationship* and secondarily a model of *the stewardship of spiritual gifts* in body life. Stewardship of right relationship is the development of "growth groups," small cells of all men or all women with high accountability in attendance, devotional reading, and prayer for each other. After starting my first growth group in 1988, I got so excited about what was happening that I shared it with my wife and with several friends. Suddenly and spontaneously, without warning or plan, ten groups of four to six people were meeting regularly. At that point I realized that it might be a good idea to provide some general guidelines for groups, including general helps for facilitating and a sampling of devotional resources. This was the extent of the "formal" managing of this growth group ministry.

Within three years, we saw the expansion of this organic movement to sixty groups. Bear in mind that there was no intent to add or multiply groups, but that is exactly what happened. And to this day, whenever I train for more than one hour on this subject of living in accountable, grace-filled relationships, similar small groups spawn as a result! I lost track after this happened nearly fifty consecutive times. When people hear about something lifegiving in nature, they want to be a part of it. They do not wait for a leader to ask them, nor do they wait to be placed in a group of someone else's making. They usually go out and start their own group with friends, that is, in their *oikos*, or household of extended relationships. We saw body life, or, if you will, first-century "church," happen before our very eyes.

Leadership for this movement is usually a shared process, since everyone has to miss a week now and then. In fact, leadership is not the point here; rather the aim is living organically, that is, in life-sharing, life-giving relationships. Also, because different people share in leadership, the stewardship of spiritual gifts takes place naturally as well. Since no group is dominated by one person leading, whatever gifts are present in the group are commonly exercised. Depending upon the gifts, people in the group are powerfully loved (teaching, mercy), encouraged (exhortation, pastoring), taught (teaching or prophecy), challenged (prophecy), served (service, helps, hospitality), or led to specific applications (leadership, exhortation), just to name a few functional results. We can call this organic process "body life ministry"!

Recall the words of organic seed maestro Larry Sallee's in chapter 4: "He knows that the multiplication of the crops depends upon the healthy interaction of all the seeds in the community." So it is with these life-sharing, gift-sharing groups where people can go deeper into God's Word, exercise spiritual gifts, share needs and pray for each other. Such activity is contagious, and thus multiplication happens by the very nature of the activity. I have found that the same process works if you invite one or two non-Christians to join a group of two or three Christians. The Spirit draws the pre-Christians in very much the same way, and they begin to respond not only to the others in their group, but also begin to open up to the Lord.

According to Wheatley, there "is a vision of inherent orderliness in the universe of creative process and dynamic change that still maintained order."[14] Who ordered the cosmos or growth group or life-changing process in community life? God did that through the fellowship of his Holy Spirit. We simply get to participate in what he is already doing. Henry Blackaby's book, *Experiencing God*, is based on this baseline biblical principle. God, as composer and arranger, designed the body to be just as he desires, with abiding relationships as the core functions of life — with him and with one another. If you begin to engage in this organism, you usually find yourself caught up in what God is doing. In my CoMission years, we called it "getting caught up in the wheel of the chariot as it races by!" Neil Cole has captured some of this essence in his book *Cultivating a Life for God*.[15]

The second example where we wandered into God's organic purposes is a sample of being *a good steward of spiritual gifts* lived out in the *stewardship of relationships*. Again we inadvertently replicated both essential pieces of our New Testament stewardship model. Our surprise of joy came as we established a spiritual gifts mobilizing ministry in 1988 in our home church at that time, Heights Cumberland Presbyterian Church in Albuquerque, New Mexico. After discipling young and veteran Christians for about five years, I realized that there was a power shortage in most believers' lives, especially as it related to service. In fact, the majority of Christians seemed to view their service as comparable to time they would spend in Kiwanis, Lion's Club, or another service organization. They were "putting in time" for God.

I determined to test out the spiritual gifts idea in the New Testament. Did God really determine each believer to be just whom he wanted? Did the Spirit really empower believers in very specific ways? We set up a discovery process where people learned about spiritual gifts and body life ministry in a group setting. We talked about the priesthood of all believers, that every believer has a ministry identity and that no one's role is optional in the body of Christ. When we looked at the individual gifts in Scripture, different people presented biblical insights on each of the gifts, using for background helpful books like Wagner's *Your Spiritual Gifts Can Help Your Church Grow.*

Then, in what turned out to be the discovery of the "sober estimation" principle in Romans 12:3, we followed up the group learning process with a one-on-one interview. Participants met with spiritual gift advisors. These advisors were laypersons whose burden or passion was to help others discover their gifts and help guide them to where they could use those gifts in or beyond our local church setting. Since pastors and ministry leaders had strong feelings about their own ministries, they were not good advisors; their own agendas often biased where they would encourage people to use their spiritual gifts. In contrast, lay spiritual gift advisors were perfect because they came with only one agenda: to help people discover their gifts and potential body life fit for being good stewards of those gifts. The personal time to talk about "the sober estimation of who I am in Christ" was God's wisdom because it continued the group process at a deeper level. The stewardship of relationships was essential to the spiritual impact of this gifts mobilizing process.

The ministry multiplied explosively. People from other churches came to the second round of our mobilization process after listening to their friends share the freedom and excitement of discovering and using their spiritual gifts in appropriate places. Today hundreds of churches have used the same approach to release Christians into body life ministry. Within three years, people who were asked to be leaders in our church were *required* to know their gifts, a result of the overall impact of our mobilizing process. We also learned very soon that the process was most effectively implemented in small or cell group settings — yet another dimension of the stewardship of relationships! In addition to my own resources on mobilizing spiritual gifts[16], another helpful model for using spiritual gifts in cell groups is Touch Outreach Ministries.[17]

As other churches and ministries followed suit in developing a gifts mobilizing ministry, I came to see that any failure was usually due to one of two issues:

1) Some people would make the process into an individualized learning process and not a group interactive discovery.

2) Some people would leave out the one-on-one interview process of sober estimation, either because they did not want to train spiritual gift advisors or they did not think that ministry place-

ment needed such personal interaction.

I highlight these two reasons because each clearly shows that the rules of our first stewardship wineskin were broken, particularly on the relationship side of the equation. Gifts are best discovered in the context of relationships, and sober estimation for an individual is still a shared process that includes other believers. It is that simple. Ministry placement by gifts is not an organizational function so much as a part of body life function, a relationship-driven process! The organization may be served, but it is the body of Christ that is empowered and released! Again we have the privilege of participating in God's work as the living body of Jesus Christ.

To clarify one last time, note that the growth group process first emphasized the stewardship of right relationships and then naturally evolved into the stewardship of spiritual gifts. Second, take note that the gifts mobilizing process emphasized the stewardship of spiritual gifts but would have failed without the inclusion of the stewardship of relationships in the discovery process. In each body life ministry, the dual priorities of Acts 2, Ephesians 4:11-16, and 1 Peter 4; 10-11 were carried out! In both of these examples, we "accidentally" captured the essence of Ephesians 2:19-22 and God's household lifestyle. We are in the process of being built together to become a place where God lives — where he can live and move and powerfully have his way.

> **We are in the process of being built together to become a place where God lives — where he can live and move and powerfully have his way.**

Practicing the stewardship of who we are and where we are moves us directly into the Spirit's organic work.

Wheatley writes, "We now speak in earnest of more fluid, organic structures ... living systems possessing the same capacity to adapt and grow as is common to all of life."[18] We experienced the dynamic, fluid, explosive multiplication because we accidentally captured the stewardship wineskin and were invited along for His ride! And, as with the disciples in Act 1:8, we discovered what it meant when the Holy Spirit comes in power both through spiritual gifts and through relationships.

**Wineskin #2: The Body of Christ as Organism — Not Just Organization.** Living out the power of God amidst the relationships he provides will create this second wineskin, an amazing web of relationships that is freed from overly binding organizational constraints and from the overplay of certain spiritual gifts.

For the moment, imagine the contemporary church as a cardboard box full of various program contents, whereas God intended that his household look and function more like a spider's web. Observe the differences between the box and the web in figure 8-a:

| A Cardboard Box... | A Spider's Web.... |
| --- | --- |
| 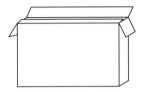 | 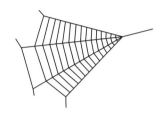 |
| ■ Inanimate object | ■ Made alive by its designer |
| ■ Self-contained | ■ Difficult to contain |
| ■ Contents can vary | ■ Variety & change normal |
| ■ Stays the same shape | ■ Can adapt & change form |
| ■ No particular importance or dependence among the component parts inside | ■ Different parts are truly interdependent upon each other to hold together and to expand |

Figure 8-a

Many of us in the West find it difficult to truly grasp the nature of this fluid life-giving organism as represented by the spider's web. Most of us have grown up in a critical thinking and organizationally minded culture. And, as we have already reflected, the church has been influenced by this worldview and our modern corporate culture; many churches are moving toward more of a business model for their structure and ministry. All these issues make it hard to even think about what we are in Christ as his body and what we can be through freedom in the Spirit. Note John 3:8 as you consider a spider's web blowing softly in the wind: "The wind blows where it will. So it is with the Spirit."

The amazing thing about such web life is that every part, no matter where or what size, is able to affect the other parts with even the smallest action. That is how uniquely interconnected the spider's web is.

Such is the same with the body of Christ: the invisible fabric of our interwoven relationships and spiritual gifts means that even a hardly noticed part of the body could take a step and influence the larger organism in ways that no one but God himself is aware! That is the importance of each and every part.

Dennis Bakke, author of *Joy at Work* and a Christian businessman, uses the illustration of a honeycomb. When building their honeycomb, bees all work together to complete this large and complicated task. In this construction process every bee's action is for the good of the whole hive.[19] It is such an environment — which for humans is built on trust, freedom, and individuals working for the good of the whole — that creates a unity and synergy that is much more than the sum of the individual parts.

Our diagram shows some key differences between the ever-dynamic web and an inanimate object. One allows for generous creativity in shape and size by the very nature of its design, the other has difficulty changing or shifting much at all. So it is with many churches whose structure is static and for whom change is overwhelmingly difficult. Wheatley observes:

> It is interesting to note just how Newtonian most organizations are. The ... imagery of the cosmos was translated into organizations as an emphasis on structure and multiple parts. Responsibilities have been divided into functions. People have been organized into functions. Page after page of organizational charts: the number of pieces, what fits where, who the most important pieces are.... We have drawn boundaries everywhere.[20]

Perhaps most importantly, though, the contents of the box — those "pieces" — are in no way dependent upon each other. Of the more than 500 churches with which I have worked in North America, the majority find their strength in multiple, independently functioning ministries that have little interface. Such is commonplace where individualism is a high cultural value. Yet the web is absolutely dependent on each part to even hold its intricate form. A web is certainly robust enough to withstand broken strands so as not to break apart, but the importance of each and every part of the web cannot be questioned! The ongoing development of such an organic design depends upon its members. Indeed, no part of the body of Christ can say, "I don't need you," because, by God's architectural design, the mutual need is shared across the whole body.

Individualism simply cannot exist in this organism, as we are made in Christ to be dependent upon one another. The interdependence is vital to healthy, long-term growth.

We are not intending to *replace* organization with organism, as some would suggest we do. Organization is an important part of any living organism. The spider's web would be in serious jeopardy of survival if its structural framework were removed. In the same way, the church desperately needs administration and organization to retain any semblance of health and order in its organic life.

However, there is a serious issue that may hinder the American church from living out its organic destiny in the new millennium. Take note of our propensity toward visionary leader-driven ministry and organizational structures straight out of current secular management models. It appears, in fact, that we are acting very much like the first-century Corinthians when it comes to overplaying certain spiritual gifts.

The Corinthians, as you may remember, loved the spiritual gift of tongues so much that they were accused of becoming "charismaniacs"! They raised that gift over others, so much so that Paul had to address the issue at length in his writing to the Corinthians. He was adamant that they see this one gift as equal with the other spiritual gifts given by the Spirit — whether or not each gift is as dramatic or emotional! Paul's words still ring out in 1 Corinthians 14:19: "But in the church I would rather speak five intelligible words to instruct others than ten thousand words in a tongue." And in 1 Corinthians 12, which chapter 4 covered in detail, Paul clearly delineates the essential importance of each and every part of the body of Christ, even to honoring those who appear to be less valued in the body.

Today it is clear that we have raised up the spiritual gifts of leadership and administration and made them "lord of the manor." Their importance in the body has been exaggerated and elevated beyond their place as two gifts among more than twenty listed in the New Testament. As demonstrated above, leadership has been so glorified that everyone believes they need to have the gift. And the visionary part of the gift of leadership has been lifted up so much that the leader's vision seems to be the only vision that matters in a local church or ministry. Administration has been raised up as organizational and management models have developed over the past thirty years — giving high praise and prominence to management by objectives, fiscal and role accountability, and other aspects of managing and controlling resources. Churches have, in many situations, gained real value through many practical helps provided. But too often the impact and focus on such organizational structuring has created a box rather than a web. Here is how a ministry partner, Bruce Lininger, sees it:

> **Often the old wineskins come as a box that exists because we do not make a sober estimation. We buy our solution out of a box sold to us at some church growth seminar, and force our people into its constraints without allowing the organic, relational process of "knowing our sheep by name" to occur.**[21]

What happens when certain spiritual gifts are raised up over others? The body of Christ gets out of balance. Certain "important" gifts are given primacy, usually to the devaluing or exclusion of other gifts. Perhaps it is like Paul's illustration of ten thousand words offered when five would suffice from the leader when sharing his or her vision. Our giving primacy to leadership, vision, and organizational language has created an imbalance that needs to be corrected.

It is time to move the gifts of leadership and administration back to their proper places in the body! We need to be led and given clear vision. We need systems guidance and appropriate controls. But in a true multi-faceted balance of body life, we also need to be encouraged — and taught. We need to balance strong leadership with powerful shepherding love. We need details clarified and administered but with helps and mercy alongside providing powerful support. We need strong prophetic words and wise discerning counsel. We must have evangelistic fervor yet also the healing of wounded hearts and physical bodies. The mutual interdependence of the body and its gifts are essential to healthy body life and growth. And God has prepared each part of his organic body to be just what is needed in the places where it is needed — *if* we are allowing effective stewardship of all the gifts rather than just one or two specific gifts that are raised up and given special position and control.

Perhaps some of you may be moved to pray one or more of the following prayers:

Lord, we confess that we have overplayed the gift of leadership. We are sorry for glorifying vision from the leader as more important than pieces of the vision you give to other members of the body — and even for glorifying that visionary leader, raising him or her up as one more important than others. Forgive us, Lord. Jesus is the only one to be raised up in glory, and we repent for doing such to Christian leaders.

Lord, I confess that I have tried to overly control the structure and functions of the church. Forgive me for exerting controls that you did not intend, even to the extreme of authoritarian leadership. I repent for trying to micromanage tasks, people, and direction in the body, at times even training people to develop the "strategic" skills that take them away from ministering powerfully through their gifts. Forgive me for this, Lord.

Lord, we stand with Jesus on the mount of temptation, seeking to release the desire to be raised up to positions of importance, to acquire great wealth or power, or to control systems and people. Help us to do this through the power of your Holy Spirit.

**Wineskin #3: Practical Steps from "I" to "We".** The move from independence to interdependence is our next strategic step. According to Peter Block, the move from self-interest to service is the critical step because it changes everything: "When we choose service over self-interest, we say we are willing to be deeply accountable without choosing to control the world around us."[22] Note that we are not using the word *dependence* here. The reason is simple: in the body of Christ, life together and ministry are the responsibility of everyone. All are to be stewards of their gifts and their relationships so that the full impact of the Spirit's work in the world can take place.

But how shall we make this move from I to We? "The first step in learning any language, including the language of potential, is to under-stand who I am, where I belong, and what part I play."[23] Max DePree's words from *Leading Without Power* provide the perfect framework for this wineskin. I call it "The Stewardship 3-Step," and it helps me move step by step into my God-prepared place in his household. Remembering initially that we bear fruit only as we abide closely with Jesus, as he stated so clearly in John 15:5, we watch for his already prepared soil in three distinct areas:

1. **The Stewardship of Who I Am**

   - Who I am affects Who We are: identifying my strengths, weaknesses, and needs is my first step of preparation for moving from self-interest to service and community.

2. **The Stewardship of Who We Are**

   - God prepared the "I" for the "We." With intentional steward-ship of team members, each one's gifts and ministry burdens may be identified and applied as a part of the team's service.

3. **The Stewardship of Who the Groups of We Are:**

   - We can discover the variety and range of gifts God has given, offering new insights about where and how God may have prepared our church or ministry to serve more powerfully.

Starting with the "I" of our existence, loneliness pervades all of Western culture. Robert Bellah writes, "American cultural traditions define personality, achievement, and the purpose of human life in ways that leave the individual suspended in glorious, but terrifying, isolation."[24] Yet as reported by Margaret Wheatley, new scientific discoveries offer a different perspective. "In the quantum world, relationship is the key determiner of everything. Subatomic particles come into form only as they are in relationship to something else. They do not exist as independent things."[25] Even secular culture is returning to a renewed understanding of the role of community and the individuals within that structure from such unexpected sources as science! Yet how much more God has given us in this regard.

My friend Nancy Boecker said to me, "You are absolutely unique, just like everyone else!" Maybe it really is not only about me. Starting with *the stewardship of who I am* confirms God's unique preparation of who I am: "For you created my inmost being; you knit me together in my mother's womb. I praise you for I am fearfully and wonderfully made"(Psalm 139: 13-14). Amazingly, I was conceived in the unity of two people, then carried in my mother's womb — He clearly prepared me for community with him and with others.

In fact, I have been designed to be a meaningful part in the body of Christ. I am a part of this fellowship of the Holy Spirit — His body — and the members are many and very diverse. God has determined me to be just who He wants me to be, with powerful spiritual gifts so that I can play my part. He has designed me also with intrinsic weaknesses, so that I will automatically understand my need for others. The next chapter very specifically identifies those weaknesses and thus reveals whom each of us needs to make us stronger.

As *the stewardship of who We are* takes shape, the I is placed into that God-prepared environment of the body of Christ. "It is not good for man to be alone," God determined very early in the history of mankind (Genesis 2:18). The body of Christ is another reflection of that biblical reality, and becomes the church in Acts. On a PBS *Charlie Rose* television interview in 2004, movie director Robert Altman quoted cartoonist Gary Trudeau: "You [the author] write dialogue for the characters so that they know who they are."[26] God the author and architect prepared us to be in community, starting with one-on-one relationships and expanding outwardly from there.

The "We" in the stewardship of who We are begins with my extended family and in my *oikos* group or ministry team, two strategic sets of primary relationships. This is where I find out more about who I am and begin to learn more of who We are — both at the same time. I learn to be faithful in relationship to those whom God brings to me, as a good steward of my spiritual gifts in those same relationships. Here stewardship becomes the real "self-interest to service" choice. It just cannot be about me anymore: "Do nothing out of selfish ambition or vain conceit, but in humility consider others as better than yourselves. Each of you should look not only to your own interests, but also to the interests of others"(Philippians 2: 3-4). In such relationships we experience the power of his resurrection, but also the fellowship of sharing in his suffering (Philippians 3: 10). Both parts are essential to understanding this reality of life together.

*The stewardship of the groups of We* brings us to the broader community to which God calls us, first and foremost so that we might worship him together. It is made up of the individuals and groups from the first two stewardship areas. Such wider community is commonly made up of multiple *oikos* groups, ministry teams, worship bands or choirs, and other groups of *We* whom God has brought together. According to Margaret Wheatley, "People need to be connected to the fundamental identity of the ... community."[27] For many of us, these "groups of We" form a church or a mission or another uniquely styled ministry, all of which are kingdom vehicles God has prepared to fulfill His purposes. If we watch carefully — make a sober estimate — at this level, we will discover that God has often prepared this larger group for very specific things. I have found whole churches with one or two primary ministry passions, but the body never knew it because they were not watching how God had prepared them individually and together.

What is essential here is that I understand that God has prepared you and me to live out who we are in the accountable community of *We* and the worshipping community of the "groups of We." Then people who do not follow Jesus will know where God lives — in us and among us — and that he desires the same for them.

**Wineskin #4: The Body Life Design Team.** Finally, as each of us practices moving from *I* to *We* in our thoughts and actions, consider three core values represented in this four-word phrase: *"body life design team."*

*Body life* means that every one of us is absolutely significant! There is nothing any of us can say, do, write, or perform that will make us more significant than we are in Christ at this very moment. There is no medal or award received, no book or play written, no achievement completed nor ladder climbed, that will make you any more important than you are right now. Because of the cross of Christ, significance is a settled issue. There is nothing left to prove and no one left to impress. Look at the words in 1 Corinthians 12:12-27 if you need a reminder of your importance. Because you are part of the body of Christ, before you fulfill any task or even use your spiritual gifts or play your part, you are special. Jesus died for you and me, and has said, "It is finished." No more striving or proving is needed. We can find grace, peace, and contentment in Christ, not in a world which demands that we always be more or higher or greater.

> **"It is finished." No more striving or proving is needed. We can find grace, peace, and contentment in Christ, not in a world which demands that we always be more or higher or greater.**

Lay down whatever it is you are trying to prove, or however you are trying to gain acceptance or approval. If you cannot lay it down, ask someone to come alongside and help you understand why it is you struggle for that acceptance or significance that you believe is just beyond your reach. "Therefore, there is now no condemnation for those who are in Christ Jesus" (Romans 8: 1). Hallelujah! We are indeed significant and settled at the foot of the cross because we belong to Jesus as full members of his body life design team.

Second, and completely separate from our settled sense of significance, is *design.* Not only are you fully and completely significant in Christ as one among others in the level playing field of the body, you also have been designed with a distinct purpose. There is no one else in the body of Christ like you, and it is God's fault! He determined each one of us to be just who he wanted us to be, according to 1 Corinthians 12:18. Not only this, but all three persons of the Trinity are involved with preparing and empowering you for your special design fit in the body.[28] There is a part for you to play in the body that no one else can play. That is how strategic you are in God's economy.

The problem for many of us, though, is that we confuse significance and role. That is, we tie our sense of worth and value to our role or ministry or position. In a culture that strongly encourages the ladder mentality, this is a very dangerous thing to do. There is no — I repeat *no*

— relationship between our sense of worth, which is already settled in Christ at the cross, and our God-designed body life roles. Our importance is already defined in Christ as complete in value, and our design is something that you and I get to be stewards of in our work, ministry, and relationships. Design means that every one of us has a part to play that no one else can play. Let us begin or actively continue the stewardship of who we are in and beyond this body life design team.

Finally, there is the value of *team*. Not only are you absolutely significant in Christ, but God also has prepared you to be strategic in his kingdom economy. Now you have a choice to make. *Team* is where every one of us chooses to seek team unity, to live out the prayer that Jesus prayed for us in John 17:20-26. Team and body life unity is not something you stumble across and say, "Wow, look what I found: unity!" No, unity and community are what we choose by acts of the will — time and time again. Philippians 2:1-5 gives us a sample of the cost of seeking unity in an individualistic, entitled, dissatisfied, sarcastic, ladder-climbing culture:

> *If you have any encouragement from being united with Christ, if any comfort from his love, if any fellowship with the Spirit, if any tenderness and compassion, then make my joy complete by being like-minded, having the same love, being one in spirit and purpose. Do nothing out of selfish ambition or vain conceit, but in humility consider others better than yourselves. Each of you should look not only to your own interests, but also to the interests of others. Your attitude should be the same as Christ Jesus.*

Paul even gives us our role model for unity — Jesus. Jesus paid an enormous price for our privilege of coming together and revealing the Father's love to the world through our relationships — a price beyond comprehension. As Philippians 2:5-8 continues, he took the form of a man and humbled himself, becoming obedient to death on a cross, the most vicious form of execution in his day. It cost Jesus his life for us to be — and stay — together in his body.

Lord, you have made us one — now please help us to keep it that way. (Do a quick checkup on your team in Appendix B.) We are all a part of his body life design team. God calls each of us to welcome every *I* to the community of the *We*.

## Conclusion

God is doing a new thing and providing new wineskins, and it involves us who are called into his community of faith. Even as he is allowing scientists and engineers to discover the interconnectedness of the world on so many levels, he is calling out his household, the body of Christ, to live organically. His calling in this season is one of coming together, and he gives us four wineskins to help in the process of coming together.

That coming together is to be manifest in the stewardship of relationships and in the stewardship of spiritual gifts, our first wineskin. Living out the power of God amidst the relationships he provides will create a second wineskin, an amazing web of relationships that is freed from overly binding organizational constraints and from the overplay of certain spiritual gifts. No longer will leaders and leadership be glorified, nor organization and structure used to wield undue control over God's purposes.

Then, to help us move from culture's "I" to the kingdom "We," the stewardship 3-step wineskin moves individuals from each one's personal design to our shared unity in primary *oikos* relationships, and finally to our worshipping community, where he is to receive all the praise and glory. Finally, we hide in our hearts the essential "I to We" phrase: *Body Life Design Team*. Each of us is completely significant in Christ. All of us also have God-designed parts to play in the body. And every one of us is called to willfully live out the *We* — choosing to be stewards of right relationships through the whole of our lives.

Such is the heart of God's New Organic Reformation.

# Chapter 7 Endnotes

1. Strauss, William and Howe, Neil. *The Fourth Turning* (NY: Broadway Press, 1997), page 7.

2. Webber, Robert E. *Ancient-Future Faith: Re-Thinking Evangelicalism for a Postmodern World* (Grand Rapids, MI: Baker Books, 1999), p 75.

3. Strauss and Howe, p 136.

4. Lininger, Bruce. Notes given as editorial feedback for this book.

5. Strauss and Howe, p 136.

6. Wheatley, Margaret J. *Leadership and the New Science* (San Francisco, Berrett-Koehler Publishers, 1999), p 4.

7. Guthrie, Stan. "Finding God in Odd Places," (*Christianity Today*, September 2005), p 106.

8. Wheatley, p ix.

9. Ibid, back cover.

10. Giller, Chip and Roberts, David. "Green Gets Going" (*Fast Company*, March 2006), p 78

11. Webber, p 75.

12. Allen, Roland. *The Spontaneous Expansion of the Church*, p 19.

13. Wheatley, p 144.

14. Ibid, p 4.

15. Neil Cole's *Cultivating a Life for God*, Long Beach, CA. Church Multiplication Assoc.

16. The Mobilizing Spiritual Gifts series is available through ChurchSmart Resource - *www.churchsmart.com*.

17. *www.touchusa.org*.

18. Wheatley, p 15.

19. Bakke, Dennis. *Joy at Work* (Seattle: Pearson Venture Group, 2005), p 85.

20. Wheatley, pp 28-29.

21. Lininger, Bruce, personal quote written as editorial feedback for this book.

22. Block, Peter. *Stewardship* (San Francisco: Berrett-Koehler Publishers, 1996), p 6.

23. DePree, Max. *Leading Without Power* (Holland, MI: Shepherd Foundation, 1997), pp 72-73.

[24] Bellah, Robert, et al. *Habits of the Heart* (Berkeley, CA: University of California Press, 1996), p 6.

[25] Wheatley, p 11.

[26] Altman, Robert, a quote during his interview with Charlie Rose on PBS, October, 2004.

[27] Wheatley, p 30.

[28] Father - 1 Corinthians 12:18; Son - Ephesians 4:7; Holy Spirit - 1 Corinthians 12:18.

# CHAPTER EIGHT

## God's Economy in Body Life Leadership

In the 1960's and 1970's, we rarely used the term leadership.... The 1980's saw the idea of leadership emerge.
Peter Block
*Stewardship*[1]

Leadership, an amorphous phenomenon that has intrigued us since people began organizing, is being examined now for its relational aspects.
Margaret J. Wheatley
*Leadership and the New Science*[2]

*But you are not to be called 'Rabbi,' for you have only one Master and you are all brothers.... Nor are you to be called 'teacher,' for you have one Teacher, the Christ. The greatest among you will be your servant. For whoever exalts himself will be humbled, and whoever humbles himself will be exalted.*
Matthew 23: 8, 10

Dave Bruskas, my pastor and friend, told a story recently. He and his daughter were sitting in the sanctuary of a church where he had formerly served. Lisa asked him a very pointed question for a child only five years old. "Dad, who is the leader of this church?"

Dave, seeing his first-ever opportunity to answer a serious biblical question from his daughter, responded, "Well, Lisa, Jesus is the head of the church, his body, and he told us that no one should be the leader because they had him, their Lord and ..."

Lisa interrupted him and said, "Dad, I know all that. I wanted to know who the 'pretend' leader is!"

Both in culture and in Christian history it took a long time for the word *leader* to rise up to prominence in the language of life and work. Of even greater interest, though, is what we are going to do about it now that the church has ordained leadership as the anointed role to guide us in the new millennium. Perhaps Peter Block, in his book *Stewardship*, speaks prophetically to us:

> This book offers an approach to reform that puts leadership in the background where it belongs. Stewardship springs from a set of beliefs that ... affirms our choice for service over self-interest. When we choose service over self-interest we are willing to be deeply accountable without choosing to control the world around us. It requires a level of trust we are not used to holding.[3]

Both Block and Margaret Wheatley, in the chapter openers acknowledge that all the commotion about leadership is a recent phenomenon. British pastor David Watson, author of *I Believe in the Church* and an early innovator in mobilizing the laity to use their spiritual gifts in the 1970's and 80's, also noted that there was no distinction between ministry and leadership in the early church. Even the Apostle Paul, in all his dominance and directness as an apostle, did not refer to leadership as the issue: "As God's fellow workers we urge you not to receive God's grace in vain.... We put no stumbling block in anyone's path, so that our ministry will not be discredited. Rather as servants of God we commend ourselves in every way ...."(2 Corinthians 6: 1, 3-4) In these three verses, Paul models what was normative language for his day — and affirms our tearing down the leadership ladder in the return to biblical language. He speaks of himself and his ministry partners as "God's fellow workers" and "servants of God," and to the work as "our ministry." The implications here again are clear: There is no leadership ladder in God's economy!

The New Organic Reformation begins afresh today as we are released from the glorification of leadership in the evangelical subculture of the late twentieth and the early twenty-first centuries. God has spoken clearly to his kingdom purposes for the equipping and releasing of all his saints for the work of ministry, and the fresh wind of the Spirit is bringing the priesthood of all believers to the fullness of their body life ministry in the world.

## Lead Like Jesus *Through* Body Life

Leadership as a Group Activity. In the West especially, we have often reduced leadership to a person — usually a single individual! My contention, though, after twenty years of watching and learning, is that leadership in the organic Body of Christ, beyond the gift of leadership itself, is actually a series of functions to be fulfilled by a group of people. Unquestionably, there are people who need to function in oversight — those whom we are to follow — but the tasks of leadership are fulfilled most powerfully by a number of gifted players, not one. (We address this essential truth more fully below.)

In the raising up of leadership as king of the spiritual gifts hill, new culturally affected trends appear that mix the organizational model with the organic model of the body of Christ. A recent book, *Lead Like Jesus*, subtly exemplifies this new pattern. As the book's summary clarifies: "We have a practical and effective leadership model for all organizations, for all people, for all situations. Jesus is simply the greatest leadership model of all time."[4] The book calls us to a high level of commitment in how we try to live out the various leadership styles that Jesus models, something the authors contend is based on our faith:

> **Your degree of effectiveness in leading like Jesus will be proportional to the quality and level that you trust in God's promises and your obedience to his instructions. If your trust**

is weak or selective, so will your ability to implement the
sometimes counter-intuitive actions Jesus calls you to do as a
leader.[5]

Before responding directly to the one concern I have with this leadership model, let me affirm that this resource has a number of helpful insights to assist us in fulfilling our ministry callings. It accurately encourages that we allow our spiritual motivations to be transformed by God at the heart level. The book also challenges each one of us to guard that neither pride nor fear steals what God desires for our lives,[6] and to realize the call for each one of us to give up our rights as servants.[7]

My one concern — a major issue — relates to the actual language of "leading like Jesus," which the book says is doable in some very specific ways. Who can do this? No one can lead like Jesus in the multiplicity of styles that he revealed through his ministry! If one of us indeed had all the ministry gifts described in the Bible and demonstrated all of them perfectly in every situation, then *perhaps* that person could

> **No one can lead like Jesus in the multiplicity of styles that he revealed through his ministry!**

indeed — powerfully and in every situation — lead as Jesus did. But Jesus did not send his Holy Spirit in power so that we could lead like Jesus in every situation. No, that is the stewardship calling of the body of Christ! In fact, we lead best and most powerfully by sharing the tasks of ministry leadership.

The church, as the body of Christ, is not *like* a body. Paul says it is the body of Christ, the organic, interdependent, many-membered representation of Jesus on earth. The full power or capacity for leadership is given to no one person but rather to a number of believers with a range of equipping spiritual gifts in his body.

We come to a primary reason why I believe Jesus and Paul did not use leadership language to dominate the ministry of the church: ministry is not about the leader but rather about effective stewardship of the body of Christ! As chapter 5 covered extensively, the action words given us were to be primarily three words other than leader: stewards, equippers, and ministers.

We can model servanthood as Jesus did. We can model the essential need for humility in laying down our wishes for the sake of the kingdom. But when it comes to the functional realities of living out the ministry of Jesus as leader, that process can only be shared by a number of gifted members of the body. Leadership is not simply for individuals who attempt to lead like Jesus in all ways, regardless of whether or not the dynamic power of the Spirit is in each and all of those actions. The body of Christ is able indeed to powerfully lead like Jesus. We have been prepared to do this *together*.

When we train Christians to adapt their equipping and leading styles to various situations, we must take care. Do we train people with definable equipping spiritual gifts to see themselves as people who can adapt their leadership style to every situation? Do we train them, as happens in *Lead Like Jesus*, to follow the purpose, values, personal vision, mission statement pattern of leading, just as we would train any business leader or manager? Do we train them to establish a "compelling vision for the organization"

> **We must take great care when mixing organic, body life models with organizational training models!**

without seeking out God's body life vision already prepared in his people's ministry burdens or passions?[8] Awareness of using such tools is helpful, even valuable in some situations. But we must take care that we pair such training with clear emphasis on the stewardship of who each person is in the power of the Spirit, with clear identification of where they are weak and who they need alongside. Without such balance, many Christian leaders will determine that they have the skills to lead without the felt need for others alongside to serve with powerful gifts in different, complementary ways. Such is the reality I see already in too many Christian ministries.

We must take great care when mixing organic, body life models with organizational training models! What if God has already determined each one of us in the body has specific spiritual gifts and ministry burdens or passions as Paul modeled in Romans 15:15-20? There is nothing intrinsically wrong with showing how different leadership styles can be utilized in every situation. There is a problem, though, if we suggest that individuals can fluidly adapt to what the body of Christ has been powerfully prepared to do only in partnership, one with another. The biblical language of stewardship, equipping, and serving suggest a different representation of leadership than one that may actually lift up the individual as capable of fulfilling the varied leadership styles Jesus portrayed at different times. Dennis Bakke offers an important biblical insight:

**Stewardship is a concept that assumes the resources we are**

using belong to someone else. We are protecting them, taking care of them, making them useful, all for the rightful owner.[9]

Jesus is the rightful head of his body, with full ownership of the dynamic power that resides therein. Stewardship language fits the intent of how his body life ministry is to be carried out in leadership. Leaders cannot lead like Jesus across the board because they simply do not have the supernatural capacity to do so! We can train people to utilize specific skill sets, and to adapt to different situations, but we cannot train them to have body-life-determined, Holy Spirit-empowered dynamism! The temptation to depend upon our learned skills is just too great. I have worked with thousand of leaders who have been trained this way whose guilt quotient is much higher than their "...level of trust in God's promises and obedience to his instructions," to use words from *Lead Like Jesus*.[10] How easy it would be if we could make leading simply an issue of following instructions. We simply cannot train people to have the dynamic power of the Holy Spirit!

God has reasons why stewardship of body life ministry — not leadership — is the biblical model for the church. God's call on our lives involves both being good stewards of our spiritual gifts and our relationships (see chapter 6). As we learn to be stewards of how God has made us powerful through our gifts, we no longer have to try to be all leadership styles to all people, adapting to every different situation and need. We learn to bring others alongside who are powerful in the ways that we are not. The stewardship of right relationships is about more than just getting along and experiencing unity. It reveals the supernatural unity in the Spirit as noted in Ephesians 4:16, "as each part does its work." As we learn to partner in ministry leadership, both in power and in relationship, we allow the work of the Spirit to dominate and direct the process or situation. Organic situational leadership brings body ministry gifts and relationship to bear. We are not raising up individuals to lead like Jesus but releasing stewards and equippers who interdependently reveal the life and power of Jesus Christ on earth.

> As we learn to be stewards of how God has made us powerful through our gifts, we no longer have to try to be all leadership styles to all people, adapting to every different situation and need.

The result? Together we lead like Jesus, and we also love and encourage like Jesus. We call out others, evangelize them and equip them — just like Jesus. We show mercy and serve — just like Jesus. We again return the leadership gift back to its body life position as one of the equipping spiritual gifts. It can be used to prepare the many-membered body of Christ to extend itself into the world through its growing unity and maturity spoken of in Ephesians 4:13-16, "... *as each part does its work.*"

Consider a ministry situation in China, observed firsthand by a friend. "In the past, most leaders were mentored relationally by older pastors who had suffered much. In the 1990's, doors opened to Western-style training. Now Chinese leaders report: "After graduating ten batches of students [i.e., training them with the 'right skills'], quality is diminishing year-by-year. Students finish with big heads but little hearts.... These schools are institutional factories producing talkers who cannot shepherd the flock. We don't want them!"[11] Teaching effective leadership skill sets may not be the answer.

Also consider our Korean friends, most of whom learn multiple skill-set training models and are expected to individually establish and lead new ministries with strategic effectiveness and power across every circumstance they face. They are expected to be "all things to all people," and are often shamed or dishonored when they prove unable to accomplish that. Remember the Korean pastors in my class at Fuller. Their greatest realization and the linchpin to freedom in Christ for them as leaders was the acknowledgement that, by God's design, each of us not only has powerful, gifted strengths, but also intrinsic weaknesses — so that we need others. They found freedom in not having to be all and do all, since alone no one can truly lead like Jesus. The Chinese believer Watchman Nee brought me to my knees with this foundational leadership principle:

> Alone I cannot serve the Lord effectively, and he will spare no pains to teach me this. He will bring things to an end, allowing doors to close and leaving me ineffectively knocking my head against the wall until I realize that I need the help of the Body as well as the Lord. For the life of Christ is the life of the Body, and his gifts are given to us for work that builds up the Body. The Body is not an illustration. It is a fact.[12]

**Primary Functions of Leadership.** My understanding of this biblical reality took on a whole new level of meaning when I developed the assessment "Primary Functions of Leadership" in the mid-1990's, and began to use it to assess leaders. After twenty years of working with Christian pastors, ministry leaders, and leadership teams, this assessment tool gave me my best understanding of the essential functions of biblical leadership. In 1 Corinthians 3:10 Paul writes, "By the grace God has given me, I laid a foundation as an expert builder." As we search further, we find out that Paul's functional capacity as an expert builder came through his three stated spiritual gifts listed in 1 Timothy 2:7 and 2 Timothy 1:11: evangelist, apostle, and teacher. He functioned most powerfully through his gift combination, which made him the "expert builder" that he indeed was.

As with the Apostle Paul, each of us has different capacities depending upon our spiritual gift blend — or gift "mooshing" as I now call it. Appendix D describes potential gift mixes related to these different capabilities. I found five leadership functions, made up of any number of gift mixes, to be primary:

- Values Keeper

- Team Builder

- Active Listener

- Vision Sharer

- Equipping Releaser

I have never found a leader powerful in all five of these primary functions! Commonly, people's spiritual gift mix makes them supernaturally powerful in two or three of the primary functions and weak in two or three. That is to say, the weak areas clarify where they need others to function powerfully with their spiritual gift combinations. God did indeed strategically design body parts to be complementary.

Steve, a Midwestern pastor, is a classic *Values Keeper*. His core value is providing a setting where non-Christians can learn about Jesus and Christianity in a nonthreatening environment. He looks at almost every issue in ministry and life through this grid, certainly biased by his gift mix as a teacher-evangelist-leader with a passion for lost people, which also makes him a powerful *Vision Sharer*. But Steve really needs an effective *Team Builder* and *Active Listener* alongside him in the ministry of the church where he is the senior pastor, because he often loses track of how established Christians are doing while he focuses on those unbelievers on his heart.

Kent, a pastor in the Rocky Mountain region, is a powerful *Active Listener, Values Keeper*, and *Team Builder*. As a teacher-pastor-discerner of spirits, Kent does not always know how to find the vision God has for his church, but when he hears vision he knows whether or not it is from God. And his leadership team and church really trust his sense of putting together the vision pieces from the body because of how he listens to people, discerns from God, and builds team. Kent really needs people around him, though, who are powerful *Equipping Releasers*, because he loses track of that important priority while focusing where he is most powerful.

Tom and Carol are supernaturally effective in their roles as *Equipping Releasers*, among other primary leadership functions in their original ministry on the West Coast and now in multiple overseas settings. Both are gifted leader-teachers who oversaw a long-term process that led to fifty new churches planted in seven different cultures. But they both need an *Active Listener* alongside so that they hear other things from God besides their own deep convictions and areas of training focus. In addition, they each need *Values Keepers* to help them stay on track to finishing well with their vision.

Debbie's gift mix of exhorter-leader-administrator enables her to be powerfully effective as both a *Vision Sharer* and a *Values Keeper* in working with leaders, teams, and various ministries in North America and Asia. She senses a clear vision from God and encourages others in that vision, but also knows where and how that vision fits into systems for practical application. But she does need both an *Active Listener* and a *Team Builder*, as she is prone to getting caught up in her vision and values. Her greatest strength belies potential weakness, which the body fills in with other gifted partners in ministry.

The real miracle of the ministry of the body of Christ is not that God raises up great leaders. It is how he mixes and matches people whose powerful strengths and intrinsic needs fit together in their leading, training, and managing of people and tasks. Again it brings us to the importance of the stewardship, equipping, and releasing of all the saints for the work of ministry. The conventional concept of leadership does not always leave room for the necessity of partnership, which my *Primary Functions of Leadership* assessment helps to clarify. This approach to leadership has helped me to understand the multiplicity of leadership functions and the necessity of valuing and empowering all different kinds of gifted equippers and supporters.

Again remember, though, that God does place leaders over us so that we all learn to submit and to live out our lives as one among many in the body. But in the sharing of leading and managing functions we learn a profoundly strategic principle: The interdependent working of

> **The interdependent working of the vision sharer, active listener, values keeper, team builder, and equipping releaser bring about greater breadth and depth of powerful ministry.**

the vision sharer, active listener, values keeper, team builder, and equipping releaser bring about greater breadth and depth of powerful ministry. It also provides a spiritual breeding ground for inviting others to play their parts and releases organic multiplication in new believers and churches. As the new players come into the process, they will see the interdependent functioning as normal body life — the rule rather than the exception. They will be able to understand body life ministry as the norm.

Some powerful visionary leaders lead from the front, those who are most visible and whom we most commonly praise. But there are also gifted social architects who know how to build and multiply ministry teams from alongside. People often praise Nehemiah for his leadership qualities of (1) surveying the ruins of the temple in Jerusalem, (2) sharing that vision with the people and with the king, and (3) praying to God. Few people notice Nehemiah 3, which has an exhaustive list detailing which family rebuilt which part of the wall or gate in Jerusalem. We do not know if Nehemiah ever touched a brick or if he was a vocal construction supervisor out leading the troops every day. It does appear, though, that he understood partnership and releasing others to play their respective parts in fulfilling God's purposes.

He obviously knew that connecting the vision to each player's God-prepared role was essential, and became a good steward and equipper of that process. Like Meg Whitman, a guiding force of the online auction house eBay, Nehemiah caught the essential reality of being in partnership with the whole community of players involved in the process — what Whitman calls the "power of us."[13] Nehemiah's advantage — and ours as well — is that we have the privilege to be stewards of the very resources of the kingdom of God found in his people, the dynamic, interdependent body of Christ!

## Steward and Equip the Body Life Design Team

We begin our wineskin applications in leadership with a review of one important passage from Ephesians and one from Romans. These passages reveal a major purpose in God's economy: the administration of his grace to the world. The first passage is Ephesians 2:19-22:

> Consequently, you are no longer foreigners and aliens, but fellow citizens with God's people and members of God's household, built on the foundation of the apostles and prophets, with Christ Jesus himself as the chief cornerstone. In him, the whole building rises to become a holy temple in the Lord. And in him you too are being built together to become a place where God lives by his Spirit.

In this new millennium reformation, God continues in his desire to live and move and have his way among us. He is building us together to become a place where he lives. Our desire in ministry leadership is to find him in our midst as we are being built together in the body of Christ, the fellowship of his Holy Spirit.

From Romans 12:1-6, we also understand that God desires to conform us more and more to the purposes of his will rather than adapting to this world's standards. As we try to (1) discern his will in our stewardship responsibility for others and, in the process, (2) equip and release the saints for the work of ministry, Romans 12:3-6 offers us helpful counsel on how to do this:

> For by the grace given me I say to every one of you: Do not think more highly of yourself than you ought, but rather think of yourself with sober judgment, in accordance with the measure of faith God has given you. Just as each of us has one body with many members, and these members do not all have the same function, so in Christ we who are many form one body, and each member belongs to all the others. We have different gifts, according to the grace given us.

So, as God is building us together, calling us to discern his good and perfect will, he challenges us first to make a sober estimate of who we are in the body — where we all function according to the grace given us in spiritual gifts.

As we begin to make practical application of the New Testament language for leading — stewardship, equipping, and serving — we start where the apostle Paul starts: we learn to be sober in our estimate of spiritual gifting, and then enable others to do the same. That is, we begin the process of discerning God's will by learning first to be watchful of what God has dynamically prepared in each one of us, moving from "I" to "we." Rather than assuming we need to figure out where and what God has for us, let us stop and take stock of what preparation he has already done in his people.

**Wineskin #5: Be Watchful Through the Stewardship 3-Step.**
As good stewards of God's grace preparing to equip the saints, start with the sober estimation of who you are as an individual (the "I"), as described in Romans 12:3, and continue from there into the "We" and finally to the "groups of We" — our "Stewardship 3-Step" process. Remember that each step builds into the next step, even as we expand our understanding of this process from the version in chapter 7:

1. **The Stewardship of Who I Am: Understanding How I Fit**

    a. Identifying my God-designed powerful strengths, weaknesses, and needs is my first step for moving from self-interest to service and community.

    b. Discovering my ministry burden or passion provides a context to use my gifts in cooperation with others in the body.

    c. When many of us do this together, it automatically leads to step 2.

2. **The Stewardship of Who We Are: Who I Am Affects Who We Are**

    a. God prepared the "I" for the "We." With intentional stewardship of team members, each one's gifts and ministry burdens can be identified and applied as a part of the team's service.

    b. We complement each other in the tasks of ministry and even find new areas in which to serve.

    c. Each one's weaknesses are identified so that others can cover powerfully in those areas, sharing in the tasks interdependently.

3. **The Stewardship of the Groups of We: Whole Church Body Life Released**

    a. Following steps 1 and 2, we can discover ministry burdens or passions that God has given across different teams.

    b. We can discover the variety and range of gifts God has given to individuals and groups; this can offer new insights about where and how God may have prepared our church or ministry to serve more powerfully.

c. We can discover how our teams and larger fellowships fit into and provide direction for our whole church.

By learning to be watchful in all three areas — the stewardship of *I*, *We*, and *groups of We* — we will gain greater insight into what God has prepared in us while we are being built together to become the place where he lives. Learning to watch for what God has prepared first acknowledges God's economy of purpose as already in place — believer-to-believer, team members-to-team members, church teams/groups-to-church teams. It also puts increased emphasis on the priority of discovering what he has already prepared in each of the three areas. How different our process would be if we chose this ahead of the normal "what we need to figure out on our own" pattern for determining mission and objectives that dominates our organizational thinking today. What a change in understanding and even application this could make for a ministry!

> **Learning to watch for what God has prepared first acknowledges God's economy of purpose as already in place — believer-to-believer, team members-to-team members, church teams/groups-to-church teams.**

I have been practicing this process of stewardship for about fifteen years now. Watching this process across multiple cultures, I have found that there are two essentials about each person God brings to you in your ministry situation. Both are included in the idea of ministry identity presented in chapter 6. Each can be used with equal effect across any of the Stewardship 3-Step areas.

The first vital element is grasping the dynamic of your *spiritual gifts*, approached from a number of different angles. The second non-negotiable element of ministry identity is *ministry burden or passion*. Chapter 9, about discerning body life vision, covers this at length. This process is based on material from my workbooks *Your Leadership Grip and Discovering Your Ministry Identity*.[14] This first part on spiritual gifts follows the categories used in *Your Leadership Grip*, including the diagram used to graphically portray the results.

As we learn to be watchful in making a sober estimation of ourselves in true stewardship style, here are six critical aspects of the stewardship of who you and I are in our spiritual gifts:

1. **What are your top three or four spiritual gifts, and are they equipping gifts, supporting gifts, or a combination of the two?** I have found that not only identifying one's spiritual gifts, but also understanding the functional nature of those specific gifts, gives tremendous insight as to how each person serves dynamically in ministry. Put simply, are your gifts more powerful in your words (equipping gifts), your actions (supporting gifts), or a combination of both? As an exhorter-leader-prophet, my spiritual gifts are all equipping spiritual gifts. A friend of mine has a gift mix of mercy, helps, and service, a sample of someone with all supporting gifts. Interestingly, 70% of the Christians with whom I have worked over the past fifteen years fit the third category: they have a combination of equipping and supporting spiritual gifts. Appendix C has some helpful questions related to this area of gifting.

2. **With your mix of spiritual gifts, are you more powerful up-front, alongside, or a combination of the two?** Here we begin to release many of you from the leadership ladder! I have discovered that about 80% of Christians find that their gifts function most powerfully alongside others, and about 20% are more powerful up-front. In fact, when released from any felt need to move up the leadership ladder, thousands of people have discovered great freedom in admitting that they are more powerful — and comfortable — coming alongside others than leading them from the front. I am an example of someone who can be very powerful leading from up-front because of my gift mix of exhorter-leader-prophet. Through this very process I have discovered that effective stewardship for me, particularly with my lead gift of exhortation, makes me equally, if not more, powerful coming alongside others in one-to-one or team settings. And even when I speak powerfully from the front as a leader-prophet, the exhorter part of me causes many people to feel as if I am sitting next to them when I speak!

After twenty years of watching body life across the whole church, I see God raising up more and more powerful "alongside equippers." Others have confirmed this same reality happening. As Christian leaders are freed from the ladder mentality, they become even more desirous of equipping and releasing others who are alongside them. These folks can be in primary leadership roles or in support of other leaders — that does not matter

— but they now understand the power and freedom of coming alongside in a new and strategic way. Their purpose is to more easily equip and release the saints for the work of ministry.

3. **What are your primary and secondary team styles?** Team Styles are the "mooshing" of your spiritual gifts, and this mix of your gifts reveals how you function powerfully in a team ministry setting. That is, what happens when the "I" functions in a "We" setting that God has prepared for him or her? The four Team Styles are:

   - Let me help you

   - Let's go!

   - Let's be careful

   - Let's stay together

   The Team Style assessment process for many people is very enlightening because it forces them to think about their spiritual gift mix in words completely different from traditional spiritual gifts language. In fact, this actually is a second angle from which to confirm a person's three or four primary spiritual gifts.

4. **What liabilities do you bring to the table because of your spiritual gifts and team styles?** Spiritual gifts do not have liabilities — but the people who use them do! A gift liability occurs when I try to exercise my gifts in my own strength rather than in the power of the Holy Spirit. In both the spiritual gifts and team style categories, potential liabilities are identified in each of the areas. Most of us see ourselves more clearly in our liabilities than anything else! Identifying our weaknesses is also essential when we work on building our ministry teams. That is, we all have opportunity to stand on a level playing field when each of us affirms not only the strengths that we bring, but also potential shortcomings. This is the most important part of who "We" are that needs to be shared and understood in a team building process. It opens the door to deeper community as we learn to receive each other even with our liabilities.

5. **What are your Primary Functions of Leadership?** What do your spiritual gifts look like in leadership language? The full range of equipping gifts, and even several of the supporting gifts, portray one or more of these five functions in multiple ways.

Your gift mix will likely reflect that you are powerful in two or three of the five Primary Functions. Having this third angle to think about how you are gifted, in addition to your Gifts and Team Style, forces you to make a more serious, sober estimate of your gifts than you have ever done previously. Appendix D has an example of which spiritual gifts relate to which primary functions.

6. **Where are you weak, and who do you need?** Not only does everyone bring powerful strengths to our team or our ministry, but we also come as needy people — by God's design. God has designed each of us with intrinsic weaknesses so that we will need others. A primary purpose in God's economy is that no one be self-sufficient! God has designed us not only to build up one another dynamically with our gifts but also to need each other in very specific ways. His economy is very efficient: the balance sheet of Spiritual Gifts, Team Styles, and Primary Functions equal out in powerful strengths and intrinsic weaknesses for each of us. Again we see the stewardship of relationships inextricably tied to gifting and how we work together in teams.

Figure 8-b shows how the three angles of gifting work together in the so-called Gifts Triangle.

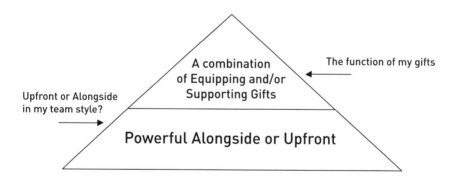

Figure 8-b

Now that we have established a method to become intentional stewards of our parts of God's household, how shall we frame ourselves in the church or ministry — the "I," the "We," and the "groups of We?" together — in leadership language?

**Wineskin #6: Moving Toward Functional Leadership Language.** Now that we have established how we can be good managers of God's household with our three-angled stewardship approach, how shall this process affect the way that we talk about ourselves in leadership? How might we level out our language so that we affirm the priesthood of all believers in the way we talk about people who function in lead roles in the body of Christ. With the ladder mentality impact on our positional style of naming ministry roles, it seems necessary to at least brainstorm about new wineskin language for leadership terminology.

Before we try out some new ideas, let us first establish a framework for our brainstorming session.

1. There is no established leadership style that is most effective throughout the Old and New Testaments. The "Moses as CEO" model did not even work for Moses, though many today are still trying to make this one work! Nehemiah presents perhaps the most effective equipping model as one who set out to be a steward of the work of all the people, resulting in the effective rebuilding of the walls and gates around Jerusalem. Yet in Acts 6 a completely different model was used to select the table servers. It appears that the primary leadership role in that situation was the Holy Spirit! No single leader was identified to lead the process of selection. Without question, a "one style fits all" approach to leadership is not appropriate.

2. As we have already discussed, the dominant words used in the New Testament in place of the leader concept were *steward*, *equipper*, and *servant*. There is no New Testament precedent for establishing leader and leadership language in the church.

3. Leadership is most powerfully fulfilled by a group of people who carry out a combination of leadership functions. My *Primary Functions of Leadership* assessment results have never revealed a leader who is powerful in all five functions.

4. New Testament language for body life is not primarily positional language. There is one head in the body, and that is Jesus Christ! There are also those whom God has placed as elders, bishops, deacons, or overseers, depending upon your denominational or theological protocol. Thus we do have spiritual oversight clearly defined. Every other body life role is wide open as far as titles and service are concerned.

5. Body life designations for believers are primarily couched in functional language as portrayed through spiritual gifts: Gifted teachers, servers, helpers and prophets, for example, are referred to as arms, legs, mouths, and so on.

6. The gift of leadership is the name of one of the equipping spiritual gifts, and that gift is given absolutely no special attention in the New Testament.

7. The ladder mentality and growing importance of calling oneself a leader seriously skews the value of using leadership language as our standard in the body of Christ.

Given this array of insights as our background, what if we took a new tack on leadership language in the body of Christ? We do not intend to get rid of leadership and its functions. But what if we moved from positional language to more functional language? Rather than running through a review of all the present terms that we use, from director to associate pastor to leader to senior pastor to executive pastor to senior associate, and so on, what if we try out one simple formula just for practice in the New Organic Reformation? Let's pretend we are going to stand against culture's ladder, if only for a few minutes, and work on an approach that is more reflective of an organic body made up completely of the priesthood of all believers.

What if we took a functional body life approach and used biblical words? We have a great deal of freedom beyond the categories of elder, deacon, or bishop, so how could we be creative? Let's use the functional language of spiritual gifts as our way of breaking out of present leadership norms: *equippers* and *supporters*. Equippers would be those who have at least one equipping spiritual gift, and supporters would be those whose supporting gifts are dominant.

> **Let's use the functional language of spiritual gifts as our way of breaking out of present leadership norms: equippers and supporters.**

What if we called senior pastors and mission executives "lead equippers"? We acknowledge their oversight role in simple terms, but keep the title focused on the function of equipping and releasing rather than on being a higher-up leader with a special title.

What if we called middle managers and leaders — directors, associate pastors, ministers of such-and-such, managers — "alongside equippers"? Again, the emphasis is on the primary functions of preparing, training, and mentoring; the "alongside" language implies that there is no concern for position other than to be one who is ready to prepare and release others to their respective equipping and supporting ministries! Such a person overseeing an area could be called "alongside equipper for small groups" or "alongside equipper for training." You must admit that people will stop and think for a minute about the functional purpose of such a role title. Such language levels the playing field in some rather dramatic ways.

**For those with supporting spiritual gifts, let's honor their function by calling them supporters!** Since there is no ladder to climb or to use for comparison, supporting functions will become acceptable and quite fashionable in the most godly of ways. And, since they are most powerful helping and serving in support of equippers, we acknowledge that function in their title. This conjures up the language used in Ephesians 4:16, *"...joined and held together by every supporting ligament...."*

What about those with equipping gifts or supporting gifts who are new Christians or just getting serious about growing in the Lord? What if we called such people apprentices or equippers-in-training/supporters-in-training?

What is the point of this brainstorming exercise? The issue is simple. Let's develop ministry language that signifies what we want to be about ministry-wise as stewards of the Kingdom. Consider that we are all equippers and/or supporters of the saints — and that quickly affirms people as players by gifting and not by a hierarchy of ministry structure. We still must take stock of character issues — modeling the fruit of the Spirit — for all of us and in every situation. But in regards to serving, what freedom we could bring to people as they focus more on using their powerful gifts and less on how to become a person of greater importance in the Kingdom!

Please, give pause for a minute. How could you change leadership language in your ministry setting that would affect an attitudinal move toward the priesthood of all believers? We validate all to be players, and we develop language for ministry roles that frees people to serve through who they are in Christ. We still affirm and follow leadership, but also create a free flow of understanding and validation of all role players in the body of Christ.

## Conclusion

God has called us, as 1 Peter 2:9 clarifies, to the priesthood of all believers, and this dramatically affects how we see leadership functioning in the body of Christ. Jesus calls us not to raise ourselves up as special — no rabbis, no teachers, no masters beyond him. He calls us who lead to be good stewards of the gifts of the Spirit in us and others. He also calls to be good stewards of the relationships that he gives us, and to equip and release the saints for the dynamic work of ministry. He calls us to service over self-interest, which removes any opportunity to climb the leadership ladder that we have incorporated into our Christian culture.

And, while there are organizational models of leadership that suggest we can adapt and lead strongly in a multiplicity of styles, this is not God's primary design for ministry. He has prepared all leaders to need others because of their own inability to fulfill all their leadership activities in the power of the Spirit.

Let us no longer glorify the gifts of leadership and administration in present-day body life! God's plan for leadership is that it be a shared process fulfilled by a group of gifted equippers who bring the dynamic power of the Holy Spirit to every situation and need. Unquestionably, we will still have overseers and people whom God calls us to follow. But the functions that need to be carried out are to be shared powerfully so that the Spirit can live and move more freely in all activities.

Given this reality, what if we first made a sober estimation of the powerful strengths and real weaknesses in every person whom God brings to our ministry, beginning first with ourselves? Each person brings a supernatural equipping or supporting capacity to the body, or, in some cases, a combination of the two. Through understanding each one's gifts and team styles — how they fit with others — we would gain new insight into how we all might serve together more powerfully in carrying out God's purposes.

In fact, what if we even adapted our leadership language to words that are functional rather than positional in nature? Perhaps this would help us to stay focused on God's purposes for each believer and be less concerned about positions, power, and personal glory.

We trust that God will bring to us new wineskins that will free us to be stewards of who we are, where we are, with greater sensitivity to how his Spirit lives and moves among us day to day through body life.

# Chapter 8 Endnotes

1  Block, Peter. *Stewardship* (San Francisco: Berrett-Koehler Publishers, 1996), p 14.

2  Wheatley, Margaret J. *Leadership and the New Science* (San Francisco, Berrett-Koehler Publishers, 1999), p 7.

3  Block, p 6.

4  Blanchard, Ken, et al. *Lead Like Jesus* (Nashville: Journeyman/Thomas Nelson Publishers, 2003), back cover.

5  Ibid, p 66.

6  Ibid, pp 26, 30.

7  Ibid, pp 58.

8  Ibid, p 75

9  Bakke, Dennis. *Joy at Work* (Seattle: Pearson Venture Group, 2005), p 37.

10 Blanchard, p 66.

11 First-hand personal account shared by an anonymous person in China.

12 Nee, Watchman. *The Normal Christian Life* (Wheaton: Tyndale House 1977), p 217.

13 Meyers, William. "Keeping a Gentle Grip on Power," (U.S. News and World Report, October 31, 2005), p 78.

14 Ford, Paul R. *Your Leadership Grip* and *Discovering Your Ministry Identity* (St. Charles, IL: ChurchSmart Resources: *www.churchsmart.com* ).

# CHAPTER NINE

## God's Economy in Body Life Evangelism

Most leaders die with their mouths open. Leaders must know how to listen – and the art of listening is more subtle than most people think it is. But first, and just as important, leaders must want to listen.

Ronald Heifetz
*Fast Company* Magazine[1]

Find out what a church's people can do and plan that, before planning its structure, forms and organization. Let the church's self-identity be revealed.[2]

George Patterson
*Church Planter and Multiplier*

But you are a chosen people, a royal priesthood, a holy nation, a people belonging to God, that you may declare the praises of him who called you out of darkness into his wonderful light.

1 Peter 2:9

If we really believed that God would show us his vision as he did for Moses with the burning bush and the Ten Commandments, would it change the way we discern vision from him? What if God reveals his purposes and direction in ways that we do not plan? What if he brings growth in unexpected ways and we miss it because we were too busy fulfilling our vision in other areas? What if God gives body life vision beyond that which he gives periodically to visionary leaders?

Janet Williams, a partner in ministry living in Europe, wrote an email recently describing some unexpected growth. She was growing a garden for the first time in many years and planted many different vegetables, flowers, and fruit. Then a hailstorm almost completely destroyed her garden, leaving her with an interesting surprise.

The garden looked like a total loss ... except for one plant. It seemed completely unfazed by everything: the unusually cool summer, the weeds, the snails, the poor soil, the wind, the hail — everything. I had at first thought it was a weed and had pulled it up daily until I discovered it was a patch of growing pumpkin gourds! By August, in spite of my hacking the vines back almost daily, they had climbed up the corn stalks, nestled in with the squash, and overrun the flowers in the next bed. They were threatening to take over our unplowed yard, even scale the wall of our house!

These pumpkins take to south Germany like kudzu takes to Georgia and Alabama red clay. They grow with complete abandon, enthusiastically, and with determination. Nothing stops them. They are unfazed by adverse growing conditions. They don't require care, water, fertilizer, talking to, ANYTHING! They just grow. I looked again yesterday; the vines are still producing![3]

## Watching for God's Vision and Movement

Sometimes God brings explosive, vibrant growth where we were not planning for it! How can we become more intentional in discerning his plans? How can we discover his heart for reaching our world in ways that he has already prepared?

Consider a thought in section I, that the church has developed a common expectation for its spiritual leaders. They are to be the visionary leaders who, like Moses, are able to go up the mountain, distill the vision from God's tablets, then return and share that vision. Why is it that, most of the time, the leader's vision is the only vision that matters in the local church as well as in other ministry or mission organizations? What if God reveals himself to the body of Christ in local ministries more regularly than just to individual leaders?

One of the primary traits of the gift of leadership is the supernatural ability to determine and communicate clear vision from God. But, with the impact of the ladder mentality virus in American culture and the glorifying of leaders and leadership roles, the visionary leader concept slowly became an expectation for anyone who fulfills the lead role in a church, ministry, or mission. Could it be that we have overplayed our hand with the vision card?

What I have discovered after twenty years of watching leaders is this: many leaders with equipping spiritual gifts are able to communicate and implement vision powerfully, but only those with the gift of leadership are able to originate vision on a consistent basis! For many leaders — at least 60 percent of those in present spiritual leadership, according to surveys by George Barna, George Gallup, and me — this is a huge problem. Consider the result of such expectations that we place on leaders, that of being the visionary leaders without the gift of leadership. They deal with tremendous expectation and guilt for not providing that which God did not include in their design specifications. Thankfully, though, there is more than one way to identify vision from God.

Active listening is a fundamental issue even for those who have the spiritual gift of leadership. One of the traits of the gift of leadership, undoubtedly, is supernaturally discerning vision from the Lord. But the vision origination is but one piece of the gift. Enabling others to carry out that vision is another part of this gift's powerful capacity, among other equipping qualities.

Surprisingly, I have found that the worst listeners in any ministry usually are those whose clarity of God's vision is strongest. In other words, those with the gift of leadership often think they do not need to listen because they know that God has already given them the vision! However, any leader who actively listens and watches for God to show up will see many things he or she did not plan on seeing, and such things will add to and sometimes change their sense of vision from God.

Since no one person is able to lead like Jesus, no one person in the body — even those with the spiritual gift of leadership — is able to clearly discern all of God's vision for any given church or other ministry! When I began using the *Primary Functions of Leadership* assessment, people commonly asked why I included "active listener" as one of the five essential leadership functions. If we take seriously Romans 12:3 and the importance of sober estimation, it should be clear that active listening and watching are essential for any leader to catch all of God's heart for their whole ministry. As Nehemiah shows us, it is crucial to actively watch what God is doing in people's lives and specific situations.

A formative moment in grasping this principle of learning to be watchful came through Chuck Smith, founder of the Calvary Chapel movement in North America. I attended an event in 1994 where he was featured on a panel with two other well-known mega-church pastors. The other two gentlemen were dressed in business suits, with Chuck in between them wearing one of his trademark Hawaiian shirts.

> **Since no one person is able to lead like Jesus, no one person in the body — even those with the spiritual gift of leadership — is able to clearly discern all of God's vision for any given church or other ministry!**

Each of them made an introductory presentation about their respective ministries. The others spoke first, giving more formal, outlined overviews of their ministry, leadership structures, and methods for growing their churches. They exemplified the already growing influence of mixing biblical and business principles for kingdom growth. Then came the unexpected in Chuck's sharing. In humility he spoke of how profoundly God was using the other two leaders and how he felt that he did not fit on the same panel. Then he gave no more than a ten-sentence summary of his style of serving the Lord, which I summarize below:

> I really don't have much of a plan. I try to watch for places where God is already working and then focus energy, people, and money toward those ends. I also like to give other people chances to see what they can do in using their gifts. They are so different from me, and it is fun to give them some responsibility and freedom and see what happens.[4]

The understated quality of Chuck's words was almost laughable at this point, as God was already using him to lead a movement that reached tens of thousands of people who do not fit into conservative and traditional churches.

What really caught my attention, though, was his idea of watching for where God was already at work. Chuck understands and lives out the principle of equipping and releasing others. He understands himself to be an equipping releaser and not a great leader, as indicated by the humility in his introduction that day. His understanding of the spiritual reality of watching for where God is already at work led him to make serious investment of people and resources in those places.

**Wineskin #7: Listening to Those Whom God Brought to Discern More Clearly What God Intends.** As some Christian leaders seek God's vision for their respective ministries, they stop and listen to other people because they believe God will give them the vision if they seek him individually. Like Moses, they presume that they, too, can climb the mountain, find God, and bring back the clear words and vision from God. This visionary leader concept took off in evangelical culture, but the ministry of soberly watching those in the body of Christ took a back seat. This aspect of ministry was most often left out completely from the vision process.

This idea of watching and listening for God's heart in the body of believers, though, is our second cornerstone piece of the ministry identity puzzle. It is of equal importance to our powerful spiritual gifts. (For those of you who want to know more about this second concept, please check out the *Discovering Your Ministry Identity* workbook for assessing ministry teams.)[5]

I call this watching and listening *ministry burden* or *passion.* Spiritual gifts are the supernatural "how" God has prepared in us to serve; ministry burden or passion is the major setting for using those gifts. It sets the primary context or activity in which we seek to use our spiritual gifts. It is a burden in that it weighs heavily on one's heart and simply will not go away. But it is also a passion for which Christians are willing to give up their very lives!

My driving *ministry burden or passion* is to invest my life in national leaders from non-western cultures. During my third trip to Russia in March 1995, I was the subject of an attempted mugging in the Moscow subway. The experience deeply disturbed me, and I realized, for the first time in my life, that I could lose my life pursuing my ministry burden of training young Christian leaders who will lead Russia into the next generation. However, amazingly this did not matter to me. I would not — I could not — stop traveling and investing in these young gifted pastors, evangelists, leaders, and teachers. That is an example of God-given ministry passion!

Most Christians are not aware that they have such a ministry burden or passion because Christian leaders have not validated this to be true in their lives. After presenting this concept biblically from Romans 15:15-20, where Paul reveals his passion for reaching the Gentiles with the gospel wherever they are, I have found that more than 80 percent of the people within hearing distance immediately begin to identify something special that God has placed on their hearts. Following are some common examples of ministry burden or passion:

- **A special activity or pursuit,** often related to one's spiritual gifts, for example, teaching, feeding the poor, visiting the sick, sharing the gospel regularly with non-Christians.

- **A specific group of people,** for example, blue-collar workers, university students, single moms, the elderly, men battling AIDS, post-modern thinkers, computer geeks.

- **A specific location,** from a very specific location to a broad area, for example, your apartment building, your university, a certain city, the village region of southern Kazakhstan, all of Russia.

- **A mixture of categories:** migrant workers in your city, Arab students in your college, teaching pregnant teens in your inner city, soccer moms (or dads), or band parents.

The options are endless because of the size of God's heart for reaching his world with the good news of his son! These lists help offer a clear idea of the breadth and depth of what God has placed on the hearts of his people. God's plan includes literally thousands of burdens and passions so that together the body of Christ can reach the world. Such is God's economy.

Some years ago I worked with the program ministry staff of a large Midwestern charismatic church. There was a team-building event that included the chance for everyone to share their respective ministry identities with one another. The plan was for each to become better stewards of who they are in Christ through the process. The last piece of the team-building was for each of the fifty people to share their ministry burdens or passions around the room, one by one, and then for the senior pastor to communicate his heart and vision for the church. Every person shared briefly, and the intensity and excitement in the room grew with each person. Christians do not have to be trained to have ownership of vision if God has already prepared hearts to be passionate! The pastor was truly overwhelmed, in part because he had never given people the chance to share their passions. His active-listening ears perked up. Because of this sharing time, new ministries began as the pastor recognized that the vision for this church included some new dimensions that God had already placed on the hearts of key leaders in the church.

Surprisingly, some people did not share about what they were actually doing in ministry, but rather in what or who they wanted to invest themselves. Their ministry burden or passion extended beyond their job descriptions and ended up reshaping portions of the church's overall ministry. Out of this sharing time, the stewardship steps for some people actually meant a change in area of service. When Christians listen to God before they plan — through the people he has brought — they may end up discovering brand-new pieces of God's vision for their ministry or mission! George Patterson's chapter opener: "Find out what a church's people can do and plan that, before planning its structure, forms and organization. Let the church's self-identity be revealed."

> **When Christians listen to God before they plan — through the people he has brought — they may end up discovering brand-new pieces of God's vision for their ministry or mission!**

What was equally amazing in that large ministry team setting, though, was the interaction as the group shared around the room. Five people in the group had the same ministry burden, and none of them knew it! This group had never shared what was on their hearts like this, unfortunately a common situation among the body of Christ.

There is an important learning point for many of us here. Most Christians do not think in "vision" language. American Christian culture asserts that vision is for leaders; thus many Christians assume that they have no vision because they are not leaders.

However, I have discovered that every Christian has at least one ministry burden or passion. While Christians often find it difficult to share vision, they can share their ministry burden or passion if given (1) clear biblical examples and sample illustrations of such; (2) validation that this is something that God really has done in them, and they do not have to be a leader or a pastor for such to be true; and (3) some time to reflect and pray, the latter especially for those who are not certain or the concept is new to them.

In this, I discovered the following principle: If you ask people who or what is on their hearts, and they think you really want to know, they will tell you. The problem is that most Christian leaders in every type of ministry simply do not ask!

You will find different actions and reactions when people begin to grasp their potential ministry passions. Some will be confirmed in their area of burden or passion and are already active there. Rejoice with them! Others will share something new and want to take steps to move from where they are into this new area. If there is support among your overseers about its viability, try to provide any needed equipping or preparation for fulfilling this ministry activity. If it is not possible for them to do this in your setting, help them find another ministry context. Joining the prison ministry of a parachurch group would be such an example, as many churches will never start their own prison ministry.

However, note that for up to 20 percent of those discovering what may be on their hearts, their ministry burdens will have to wait for fulfillment. For a number of people, it is not God's timing at present for their particular passions. Others are not yet ready for what God has placed on their hearts, and some other preparation is necessary as they wait. And for many Christians, there are times when God simply wants them to learn how to follow before they lead or serve in a new area of burden or passion. Submission and an attitude of servanthood are essential prerequisites for releasing people to their ministry passions.

This happened in my own life. I wanted to move into missions immediately after my ministry training, but God clearly called me initially to five years of youth ministry — not on the top of my heart's list. But in those years of preparation, I learned to teach biblical concepts in simple terms, which was crucial for working with junior high and high school kids. That training has become indispensable to my work in everything I have done since. "Wait..." and "Learn to follow..." are two famous phrases that God will use for many Christians in this process. His timing for releasing people to their heart burdens will fit his economy of time and not our sense of entitlement.

What about leaders who do have the gift of leadership? Do they need to learn to actively listen to the ministry burdens and passions of the people God has given in their fellowship? Absolutely "yes"; I have seen that God consistently adds pieces of the puzzle to the vision already given to that lead equipper. I once worked with a ministry team where the lead equipper had a team of people with whom he had worked for ten years — a surprising fact considering that there were eighteen people in the room! He was a brother who really knew his players.

> He practiced the "ministry of sober estimation," not only in becoming a good steward of the gifts of each of his team members, but also in listening to their hearts.

As we closed our team-building time, each person briefly shared his or her ministry passion. The lead equipper was certain there would be no surprises since he knew everyone so well. Suddenly, the person in the room he knew best, other than his wife, shared a burden that caught him completely off guard. He had never asked her — someone he knew like a sister — what was most on her heart. Hearing that one ministry burden soon facilitated a major change in the overall direction of that church.

This happened because the lead equipper was willing to watch and listen. He practiced the "ministry of sober estimation," not only in becoming a good steward of the gifts of each of his team members, but also in listening to their hearts. From that process, God gave new and extended vision. No leader in any ministry setting has a monopoly on the vision market.

I have developed a folksy diagram to illustrate this principle, which I call the "double umbrella principle" (see figure 9-a). We are actively applying the "Stewardship 3-Step" concept to the vision area of body life ministry where watchfulness is essential. Learn to listen for vision through the ministry burdens and passions of those people whom God has brought among us — individuals, groups, and even the whole church gathered.

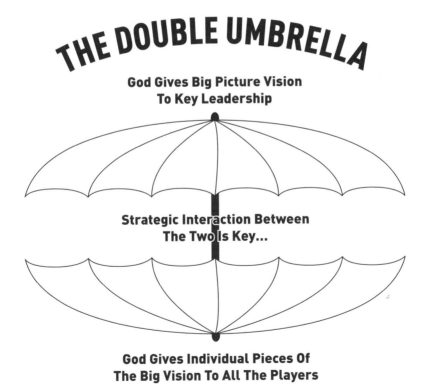

# THE DOUBLE UMBRELLA

**God Gives Big Picture Vision
To Key Leadership**

**Strategic Interaction Between
The Two Is Key...**

**God Gives Individual Pieces Of
The Big Vision To All The Players**

Figure 9-a

Take note of the unusual configuration of the two umbrellas. The top umbrella reflects the lead equipper's vision and what has been shared and assimilated with input from other leaders and equippers in the church — as exemplified by the two illustrations above. That is, the "I" and the "We" formulate their shared vision, and then they provide opportunities for people in the larger body — the "Groups of we" — to understand the principle and share their hearts. In an open church setting, members from the whole body share first, that is, individuals who have a ministry burden. People are asked to share something in which they are willing to invest their lives, not what they think the church or mission ought to do. It is imperative that each must take ownership for what is shared or else it simply becomes a meaningless exercise that will never be lived out.

As members of the body share, their input forms the bottom umbrella. In the ensuing strategic interaction, the equipping team often gains new insights to enhance the overall vision of the body. How does the content from the top "vision umbrella" fit with the bottom "ministry burden umbrella"? It is hard to find a more potent learning environment for discovering God's heart in a ministry than one like this!

Following are some general guidelines for an effective way to start this sharing process. Someone presents the ministry burden or passion concept biblically from Romans 15:15-20.[6] Following that, several hand-picked people who are able to clearly articulate their ministry burden or passion begin to share. This ensures that people truly grasp the principle and are better able to personalize it. After people from the larger group have the opportunity to share, several from the team of equippers share their burdens, and then the lead equipper lays out his or her sense of vision from the Lord for the church or mission.

Here's how one local church pastor handled the process of listening to God from the whole church family, in this situation about 1,100 people:

> This idea of active listening and watching the Body, to see who God is bringing and what He is doing, is a key now in what I do to help me determine vision! Recently at the end of regular services, I had people get into Circles of Five at which time I asked them guided questions and they wrote down their answers. This is one way that the Leadership Team can know what the Body is thinking.[7]

Through the process, no matter the size or shape of the ministry, the goal is to watch for God to confirm direction and purpose, or reveal something unexpected or unplanned. If people are open, he usually shows up and surprises everyone. Practical changes in vision and direction, if any, are applied following the community process, and practical application follows. I encourage that such a "double umbrella process" take place among the leadership team at least yearly, and that the whole community gather at least every two years. In the leadership team sharing, the lead equipper's vision is the top umbrella and team member's burdens or passions are pieces of the bottom umbrella.

Allow God the opportunity to surprise you! If you have a gifts mobilizing process where people discover their ministry identity and go through a personal interview to determine where they may fit best in serving, you have that additional source for hearing from God through the various body parts.

Consider the implications of an earlier quote from Mort Meyerson: "The way to be a leader today is different.... The essence of leadership today is to make certain that the organization knows itself."[8] Now this makes sense for the body of Christ in its local situation. The whole process of learning is what George Patterson calls the "self-identity of your church."[9] From this you will also find yourself beginning to pay more attention even to the ministry identities of new people whom God brings into your fellowship. Why? It is clear that God often reveals new or different directions through the spiritual gifts and the ministry passions of those new players.

Be watchful. Help new players discern who they are and what that means in the stewardship of who they are in the midst of your community. It will often create newness you had not planned for and also will create ownership for people investing in ministry at levels you cannot train!

Peter Block writes, "Let the commitment and the cause be the place that we work."[10] That is the strategic issue which ministry burden or passion brings to the fore: commitment and ownership for individuals playing their respective parts in the corporate body. Tom Litteer, a friend in ministry and the lead equipper in the church he pastors, First Presbyterian in Sparta, NJ, has seen this principle enacted with some incredible results in their church. Tom and the elders have given license for people to actively pursue their ministry burdens or passions. Here is a sample of heart burdens that were given the support to become viable areas of ministry and have born real fruit:

- "Soul Cafe": a nursing home ministry

- Intercessory Prayer Team, which has led to a number of "Prayer and Healing Teams"

- "Pyro Worship": a new worship service reaching out to middle and high school students and young adults in the community

- "Loving Arms": a ministry to unwed moms who are considering placing their children for adoption

- HUD apartment complex outreach: includes worship, a craft night, and a game night, as well as adding an intern to be a spiritual presence on site

- Sunday School: a new young couple has come in with a new vision for this area, and people are rallying around them [11]

Tom writes:

Some of the ministries evolved or were created by those who were already spiritually mature, others by those who were growing in their faith to the point of feeling the urging of God to start something new. In fact, a number of our new elders have come from these growing believers. We watched how they mentored and encouraged others in their new ministry, and whether or not they had a humble heart. None of these ministries came from some kind of strategic plan set out by the elders or some other group.[12]

The elders not only were intentional in being good stewards of both spiritual gifts and ministry burdens. They also were good stewards of relationships as they watched for new elders in their fellowship by watching the way those potential overseers handled relationships in their new ministries.

Note that these applications — that of practicing the double umbrella principle to discern God's body life vision and in helping people to discover and fulfill their ministry burdens — can also be executed in churches that are small group or cell-based. As Margaret Wheatley writes, "Body life means that we include more and more eyes."[13] In fact, I have seen scores of small groups where God has given a whole cell the same ministry passion to fulfill together. This should not be surprising in a living cell of the organic body of Jesus.

The lead equippers in a church can also meet with small group shepherds as another forum to listen, watch, and discern God's heart for the whole fellowship as represented through those small group equippers. However, freeing groups and individuals to try out new things is a process that must first be learned. Litteer adds: "We are still in the early stages of learning permission-giving." There is indeed much to learn in choosing to actively equip and release the saints to the work of ministry in this new way. Undoubtedly this process has its messes and failures, but the fruit that is born reveals that God has indeed prepared his people with things that come from his heart and perhaps not from the church's mission statement.

**Wineskin #8: Watching and Listening as Overseers.** Let's extend our discussion of watching and listening for God's heart and vision to elders, deacons, church counsel, or executive board — whoever is positioned as the decision-making team in your church, ministry, or mission. No matter how you structure your board of overseers, consider this one change in the role description: given our new understanding of Romans 12:3 and the ministry of sober estimation, call the board members "watchers" and free them to do just that: watch and listen.

We spend so much time leading, directing, and voting that sometimes — maybe most of the time — we forget to watch for God working amidst all the people, from the "I" to the "We" to the "Groups of We." Nehemiah gave us an inspiring model of overseer ("watching over") as he surveyed the ruins and listened to the people in his preparation for managing the rebuilding of the walls of Jerusalem. Yet the closest we often come to watching is when we request written reports on various ministries! What if we saw the ministry of sober estimation as an essential function in watching for God to show up in new and different ways in the midst of our churches and ministries?

What if we trained and released our executive team or overseers to:

- watch for new wineskins — where the Spirit of God is moving in new ways through the lives and actions of various members in the body?

- watch the big picture — what we hear and see God saying through the things happening among us and even beyond us in small pockets.

- watch spiritual health issues — going out to lunch once a week with someone new in the body just to watch and listen to their heart and their spiritual health.

- watch for lies and untruth — and address the issues as they happen.

- watch that people are being cared for in their *oikos* settings.

- watch for new ministries that alongside equippers may want to start — even set up a process where they come to you when they have a new ministry burden on their hearts.

- watch for organic growth — unusual places where the Spirit is doing something special or new or different.

Wonderful things can happen when people quit talking and really watch and listen. They can suddenly see things that were there but they missed because they were not wearing their watching glasses or using their active listening ears!

Some may object, "But I cannot do this watching unless I am spending time with people in our ministries!" Perhaps that should be a part of the watchers' primary commitment: to meet once a week with different people in the body. This does not mean simply meeting with people on a committee that an elder oversees. This is about broadening out to meet with people all over the body to listen to their hearts for ministry, to discern how they are growing, and even to identify new elders who are mentoring other believers through their new ministry or new cell.

How can you release your elders or leadership council to be watchers? What difference might this make in discerning God's heart for your city, your church, unbelievers, special needs, or other important issues or situations? The prerequisite is trusting that God has prepared his people to be just whom he wants. Learning to give permission, providing the needed training, and even cleaning up serious messes will all be a part of the learning curve. But do not doubt that God's economy has this design for body life: he has prepared the players to be ready and willing to play their impassioned parts in ways that we did not plan.

## Breathing Life into a Darkened World

According to Robert Webber, "The challenge in a postmodern world is to be the presence of a transcendent reality here on earth, the embodied community that draws others into participation in his incarnate presence, the church."[14] How can we do that?

Our new wineskin for evangelism (#9 on next page) repeats a

recurring theme that began in chapter 5. The key to effective evangelism is choosing to be a good steward of God's power in me — my spiritual gifts — in the context of relationships in which God places me. Because God has prepared me to be powerful according to his design features for

> **The key to effective evangelism is choosing to be a good steward of God's power in me — my spiritual gifts — in the context of relationships in which God places me.**

me, and will consistently bring me to the people in whom he wants me to invest, the opportunities for impact are already in place.

Acts 2 describes the wind of the Spirit of God poured out in power. It came through spiritual gifts in the tongues of many languages.[15] The people gathered were from many different places and yet each heard their own tongue from the mouths of the disciples. Peter helped them understand what had happened and called them to repentance in the name of Jesus, and thousands responded.[16] From that point, the other powerful work of the Spirit, that of creating a community of joy and sharing, drew in new believers daily.[17] The Spirit was revealed both in the exercising of powerful spiritual gifts and in the lifestyle of a grace-filled community. People were moved to response by both, with the power of the Spirit revealed in Peter's calling them to repentance in Acts 2:38. This is a powerful account of body life evangelism.

However, the focus has too often been primarily on the verbal witness in Acts 2: 38-41 — Peter's words that resulted in many conversions. That is what we often understand to be the real strategy of evangelism. We assume that the right words proclaimed will cause response. For organic reasons, we are going to concentrate our attention on the powerful gifts exercised before and the authentic community growing after Peter's convincing, Spirit-empowered proclamation. Therein we find the key to reaching the world for Christ today.

**Wineskin #9: Evangelism — Be Who You Are Where You Are.** Remember the cultural challenges in section I: Christians look a lot like the world today. Non-Christians may hear our verbal witness but then look at our materialism, corporate ladder climbing, and exclusive politics.[18] The phrase "Your actions speak so loudly that I cannot hear a word you say" reflects a common attitude in our postmodern world. People are looking for authenticity and truth revealed in real people and genuine relationships, where the message and the messengers have the same integrity.

What do we have to offer? First, each of us is powerful in the Spirit in very specific ways through our gifts. Learn to be who you already are in the power of the Spirit! God saves us by his grace, then gives us his power in our particular gift mixes so that we each can serve others, administering his grace in its various forms.[19] As shown in Acts 2:1-8, the authentic role of ministering through spiritual gifts is to powerfully translate the gospel in personalized ways that people can understand. It is the love of Jesus translated through grace-filled people who make up his body.

> **The authentic role of ministering through spiritual gifts is to powerfully translate the gospel in personalized ways that people can understand.**

With unbelievers, in fact, using our gifts becomes our most supernatural means of serving and loving them. Being who we are in Christ reflects the essence of his grace in ways that are far beyond our natural capacities.

Given this, when it comes to evangelism, why then do many Christians think they have to act like an evangelist when living out and sharing their faith in Jesus? The ladder mentality and the visionary leadership myths help to encourage similar models in evangelism. The up-front verbal witness to people is usually portrayed as the most important. However, body life evangelism is not when everyone looks and talks like gifted evangelists, powerfully persuasive and able to be all things to all people. Instead, it is when each of us plays our body life-designed roles and the power of God is revealed through our words and actions. Paul did this by modeling the use of his gifts, and each of us is called to use our gifts to reveal God's grace. The difference is that many of us have different gifts than the Apostle Paul!

Why do I not bear the same fruit as an evangelist like Paul? Because I am not an evangelist, and it is more important that I understand who I am, not how I can try to be like Paul. Note his comments in 1 Corinthians 3:5-7, 9-10:

> What, after all is Apollos? And what is Paul? Only servants, through whom you came to believe — as the Lord assigned to each his task. I planted the seed, Apollos watered it, but God made it grow.... For we are God's fellow workers; you are God's field, God's building.

> By the grace God has given me, I laid a foundation as an expert builder, and someone else is building on it.

Paul really did understand his part in the body as a "fellow worker" — that is, as nothing more than one playing his grace-empowered part. In the last sentence he is playing out the evangelist-apostle part of who he is as demonstrated by his being an expert builder — even as he is using his third gift, teaching, to instruct the Corinthians.[20] He not only knew who he was in Christ, but also knew that others needed to understand and play out their God-determined parts.

We see now why Paul is serious about our making sober estimates of who we are in Christ. That is the first step for discerning the will of God (Romans 12:2) and it also introduces the next issues referenced in 12:4-6: body life relationships and spiritual gifts discovery. It is *imperative* that we understand how we are powerful, as Paul reveals in 1 Corinthians. Often we forget that this same principle plays out actively in evangelism and discipleship in very real ways.

Once I had realized that my most powerful style in evangelism was to be myself in my gifts, it took all the pressure off me and returned it back to God. He had already established the process to be at his determination and not mine. As an exhorter-leader, I began to spend time with non-Christians for the purpose of encouraging them. When I try to evangelize like Paul or like Peter as modeled in Acts 2, it is most often in my own strength. But when I encourage as a gifted exhorter, the power of God is revealed! Invariably, over time, when I encourage and build up people, they begin to open up about their deeper needs. I have seen this happen hundreds of times, including several stirring conversions that developed over several years of such encouragement.

With my exhorter-leader-prophet gift mix, now that I understand how God uses the combination more and more, I see God show up and give supernatural insight prophetically. Recently, I met with a young Christian very strongly affected by the individualism of our culture. He had been in and out of our church. During our lunch, it became clear that the Lord was calling to him through me, and so I spoke the words I believed were from God: very firm, very directive, and very timely. He responded openly, knowing it was indeed God speaking to him and calling him home to our fellowship. Only God can do that!

The same thing can happen to those who are not Christians. Through the prophetic gift, God gives clear, ecstatic words to Christians to say to non-Christians. And when these words *are* from God, they are received with awe and wonder. Such is the power of God when gifts are exercised in relationships, the second part of our equation, as we further discuss below.

I encourage you to not worry about trying to be the Apostle Paul, Billy Graham, or someone whom you know and respect for their evangelistic zeal and their fruit. Rather, I challenge you to soberly estimate who you are and learn to be yourself by powerfully using your gifts. God will show up, whether in your serving powerfully through shingling the roof of an unbelieving friend in need, loving powerfully with a pastoral or mercy gift, giving guidance from the word through your teaching gift when asked for advice, or exhorting others practically through a parenting workshop at your child's school. Body evangelism demands that all of us play out our gift-mix parts so that all people can be reached in your town, your region, and to the ends of the world.

Body life evangelism has a second, relational part. We use our spiritual gifts in evangelism in the specific relationships that God brings into our lives. Remember that organic body life, by design, is relational. It is being a good steward relationally with unbelievers, day in and day out as our life paths cross. It is introducing our friends who do not know Christ relationally with our friends who do know Christ. When many Christians in the same fellowship share individual investments in non-Christians, this will foster impact in shared ways. According to Roland Allen, "Spontaneous expression begins with individual expression; it proceeds to corporate expression."[21] And Watchman Nee writes, "The vessel through which the Lord Jesus can reveal Himself in this generation is not the individual but the body."[22] In God's economy, what starts with the individual can end up involving all of us!

Margaret Wheatley offers profound clarity here: "power in organizations is the capacity generated by relationships."[23] How much more power and capacity we have as members of the body of Jesus spread all over the earth, each in our God-prepared contexts. We come back to the heart of God, living out our relationship with him and one another.

> **God has prepared me to be who I am so that I can live where I am relationally by his design.**

Given this, what if God's economy has already prepared even the relationships he has brought and will bring into our lives? God has prepared me to be *who* I am so that I can live *where* I am relationally by his design. Because of this, I can use my spiritual gifts in the relationships God has brought and will bring my way. As I learn to be watchful for who he brings, I then act as a steward of each of those relationships.

Figure 9-b shows a simple chart to help you plot your God-prepared strategy:

## Investing Who You are Where You are...

- I am a good steward of my relationships, always watchful
- I am a good steward of my powerful gifts in those relationships

| Oikos/"Household" Categories | Who has God brought? | Which of my gifts fit? |
|---|---|---|
| Neighbors | | |
| Extended Family | | |
| Work associates | | |
| Close friends | | |
| Casual friends | | |
| Contacts in workout, school, job, insurance agent | | |
| Acquaintances with newness in their lives: new baby, new home, new job | | |
| The "Surprise" category: gas station attendant, store clerk, waitress, etc. | | |

Figure 9-b

First, who has God brought into your life in one or more of the categories listed? From three or four or five you identify, make a priority list as to whom you believe to be open spiritually. Second, which of your spiritual gifts are you using or could you use in each of those relationships?

Four years ago, I made an acquaintance in coffee shop near our home that I frequented. Several weeks later, we saw each other again and had another chat. Intrigued by my "spiritual" work, Alan asked many questions. The next time we met, he asked me if we could start a small group just to talk about serious life issues. Now, four years later, he and I are in a group of five men that began as three Christians and two seekers. One of those men has since come to Christ.

My coffee shop friend is still asking his many questions and still open but not convinced. In this process, I was already watchful of people God might bring, and this new friend became an obvious choice of someone spiritually open. What gift did I use to interact with him? My gift of exhortation was a real blessing in this situation, as I am supernaturally adept at encouraging others. This was just what my new friend needed — someone who was encouraging and available.

What an amazing practical reality. God saved us by his grace. He makes us powerful with specific portions of his grace gifts as he calls us to become good stewards of who we are. We then exercise those gifts in the relationships he has already prepared for us. Such organic strategy is both brilliant and simple, profound and yet doable. I call it "investment brokering," but this action strategy is so much more

> **Each of us has a role to invest who we are where we are as members of the one Body of Christ!**

important than any financial investing we may do. God has prepared the "powerful how" and the "strategic who." Each of us has a role to invest who we are where we are as members of the one Body of Christ! God has so placed each one of us that, together, every day, we can watchfully broker his investments, both gift and relationship.

What is equally incredible here is that God desires that we share our relationships through body evangelism. We do not have to be in this alone, the common model in America. This is another example of the *oikos* principle — our friends, our household. As we commonly share our lives with Christian friends, we now can discover ways to share our Christian friends with our non-Christian friends. As our prebelieving friends watch how Christians live out their love relationships together, they will see Jesus in the commitment, the servant attitudes, the openness, and the shared fun!

If you are willing to be a good steward, then broker your relationships for the sake of the kingdom! When conversion is understood to include relational investing and even conversion into community, it changes everything about evangelism. The group of men mentioned above grew from two to five. That happened for this very reason of brokering friendships — sharing relationships with each other. Alan Fowler, my coffee shop friend, invited a spiritually seeking friend of his, and I invited two Christian friends of mine. We — and our wives — have begun to live this *oikos* evangelism as an extension of our lives in our church.

We are also realizing the power of this *oikos* investment brokering as a church. Several months ago our pastor, Dave, and I sat down to evaluate God's relational strategy as he has organically developed it in the first five years of our church plant, City on a Hill Fellowship. We asked this question: What has God done relationally that we did not plan during these early years of living out our witness through the Lobo Theatre on Central Avenue in Albuquerque?

We have seen people come to Christ and grow deep through our life groups. We have seen relational investment at several grade schools and middle schools in the so-called "war zone," through which youth have accepted Christ and are now in our youth group. That group of young adults has a unique multi-ethnic flavoring and is reaching across boundaries in ways that we could not have planned. Every Thursday night, we spend time with drug addicts and AIDS victims on Central avenue, developing friendships with them. Relational investing also occurs with University of New Mexico students and through the East Central Ministries. In Appendix E, Dave paints a picture of what we are learning about relational evangelism at City on a Hill Fellowship.

Our church is learning to be watchful of what God is doing in his economy so that we can be more intentional in both the using of our gifts and the sharing of our non-Christian *oikos* relationships. In our youthful learning, God has waited patiently for us to understand the nature and purposes of his investment-brokering plan, our body evangelism role as a community in Albuquerque, New Mexico.

## Conclusion

Learning to watch for God at work is crucial for discerning vision and doing evangelism. God provides vision not only through leaders but also through the ministry burdens or passions of the other people who make up churches, missions, and ministries.

Another key is to be observant of people already in our lives who need Jesus. God, in his economy, has already placed those people there. We do not have to be Billy Graham or Luis Palau to reach people in our individual lives, because God has collectively prepared us with the gifts needed to be powerfully who we are with the people he has brought into our *oikos* relationships — our households, our friends.

# Chapter 9 Endnotes

1  Heifetz, Ronald. "The Leader of the Future," (*Fast Company*, June 1999).

2  Patterson, George, "The Spontaneous Expansion of Local Churches," (article source unknown), p 597.

3  Williams, Janet. Personal story shared in an email to friends in July 2005.

4  Smith, Chuck. Paraphrased comments from a "Leadership Network Summit" in Phoenix, AZ, in May of 1994.

5  Ford, Paul. *Discovering Your Ministry Identity* (St. Charles, IL: ChurchSmart Resources, 1999), p 30.

6  A simple Bible study overview of Ministry Identity can be found in Appendix E.

7  Weldon, Steve. Personal email notes sent in as editorial feedback for this book.

8  Meyerson, Mort. "Everything I thought I knew about leadership is wrong" (*Fast Company Handbook of the Business Revolution*) pp 9-10.

9  Patterson, p 597.

10  Block, Peter. *Stewardship* (San Francisco: Berrett-Koehler Publishers, 1996), p 10.

11  Litteer, Tom. Personal email notes sent in as editorial feedback for this book as it relates to First Presbyterian Church, Sparta, NJ.

12  Ibid.

13  Wheatley, Margaret. *Leadership and the New Science* (San Francisco, Berrett-Koehler Publishers, 1999), p 66.

14  Webber, Robert E. *Ancient-Future Faith: Re-Thinking Evangelicalism for a Postmodern World* (Grand Rapids, MI: Baker Books, 1999), p 83.

15  Acts 2:1-13.

16  Acts 2:38-41.

17  Acts 2:42-47, 4:31-37.

18  Webber, p 169.

19  Ephesians 2:8-10 and 1 Peter 4:10.

20  Paul reveals his spiritual gifts in 1 Timothy 1:11 and 1 Timothy 2:7.

21  Allen, Roland. *The Spontaneous Expansion of the Church* (Grand Rapids: Eerdmans, 1962), p 15.

22  Nee, Watchman. *The Normal Christian Life* (Wheaton: Tyndale House 1977), p 216.

23  Wheatley, p 39.

# Epilogue

We want to examine leaders' ongoing response to the work of
the Father in them so that the work of God through them is
brought to greater focus and expansion.
Rick Tansey
*Maximum Health*[1]

*I will attach tendons to you and make flesh come upon you and
over you with skin; I will put breath in you, and you will come to
life. Then you will know that I am the Lord*
Ezekiel 37:6

Rick Tansey, a good friend and partner in ministry, says that
organic, life-giving ministry needs to include three overlapping areas:
leader health, structure health, and ministry health. As noted above, he
starts with the leader. Such is what I have done in *Knocking Over the
Leadership Ladder*. Life and ministry in the Body of Christ today, more
than ever before, hangs on our understanding of Rick's first axiom:
healthy leaders.

For too long, though, we have raised up leaders and leadership in a
non-biblical way. For too long we have subtlety encouraged that being a
leader is what life is all about, just like secular culture around us. For too
long, we have believed that those leaders alone are to discover a vision
for the Body of Christ that will extend God's Kingdom purposes. But
God is changing our perceptions through generational change, renewed
search for community, and growing awareness of the world's interconnectedness on multiple levels. The new organic reformation is upon us!

He is breathing new life into his people, the Body of Christ. We are
being built together to continually become the place where He lives and
moves and has His way among us. He is coming among us to breathe

new life even as we drink our stale wine encased in our cracked cultural wineskins discussed in Section I.

> The church as the realized expression of the 'fellowship of faith' will break down our extreme individualism. Modern individualism is something different from a personal relationship with God in Christ. It is a form of Christianity that fails to understand the integral relationship that exists between the members of Christ's body.[2]

He has fresh, full-bodied wine for us as revealed in Section II. Leadership is understood properly when seen in context of community and body life shared ministry. It is lived out more powerfully when the biblical imperatives of stewardship, equipping and releasing and given full sway, with a servant heart as the necessary underpinning.

Given this, please consider the new wineskins for leadership, vision, and evangelism, among the nine just presented in Section III, as ways for you to go out on a limb. My friend Peter says: "Come on. Go out on a limb. That is where you will find all the fruit!"

For me personally, I highlight four insights that have been life-changing through this process. What better way to summarize this book but to share my own life and ministry "shape-shifting" principles in the simplest of terms:

- Kingdom breakthrough happens when I am a good steward of who I am in Christ in those relationships God has already prepared for my investment. 1 Peter 4:10-11 covers it well.

- Where are you powerful and who do you need? How I wish I had understood both parts of this twenty years ago!

- I found a missing biblical principle in Romans 12:3-6: make a sober estimate of who I am and who we are. It is essential for understanding God's economy and how He works among us.

- Who I am affects who we are. Given this, let's look at who God brought to discern more clearly what God intends.

God is really smart. Let's pay better attention.

# End Notes: Epilogue

[1] Tansey, Rick. *Maximum Health Workbook* (St. Charles, IL: ChurchSmart Publishers, 20), p. 25.

[2] Webber, Robert E. *Ancient Future Faith* (Grand Rapids, MI;  Baker Books, 1999), p 80.

# Appendix A

## Discovering and Fulfilling Your...
# Ministry Identity
### ..while building your CHURCH!

**A. Paul describes who he is in Romans 15:15-20**

    1. Paul knew what his <u>  spiritual  </u> <u> gifts </u> were: evangelism, apostle, & teacher

        **....the supernatural HOW**

    2. Paul knew his ministry <u>  burden  </u> or <u>  passion  </u>: the Gentiles

        **...the God-instilled who, what and/or where**

**B. The heart issues: what is Your Ministry Identity?**

    1. How am I supernaturally empowered to function as a Christian?

        **...primary spiritual gifts**

        **...gift combination modeled in Ephesians 4:11 (pastor-teacher)**

2. For whom or what has God empassioned me, and where might that lead me?

   a. Specific activity?

      **...teaching, feeding the poor, hospital visits**

   b. specific group of people?

      **...blue collar workers, single moms, elderly**

   c. specific location?

      **...Russia, Columbia, Boston, hometown**

# Appendix B

# How is Your Team Tracking?

How does your team rate on the following team values? Use this guide as a check-up for determining the health of your leadership or ministry team.

Pick the most accurate response from the sets of two choices listed below:

| Team on Track | | Team Off Track |
|---|---|---|
| ___ Open, accepting atmosphere | or | ___ Bored or stressed atmosphere |
| ___ Discussion, with all sharing | or | ___ A few dominate discussion |
| ___ Vision/Purpose is understood by all players | or | ___ Vision/purpose unclear or confusing |
| ___ There is a general consensus about the purpose of our team | or | ___ Actions are being taken without clear unity of purpose on the team |
| ___ Each player knows role and acts accordingly | or | ___ Players unsure of their roles and there is resulting tension |
| ___ Players listen to each other | or | ___ Players do not listen to each other |
| ___ Disagreements are okay, and are common in team discussion | or | ___ Disagreements are left unresolved or are NOT okay. |
| ___ Leader shares leadership functions according to need | or | ___ Leader always the "boss" with no releasing of leading functions |
| ___ Players evaluate team's work without personal attack | or | ___ Criticism is embarrassing and creates stress. Players fear clobbering |

___ Team meetings are open for      or      ___ Creativity or honest expression
    ideas and appropriate sharing              of feelings is off limits.
    of feelings                          Feelings are thus hidden

___          **Totals**         ___


9-10 on left column = right on track.

7-8 on left column = time to address issues is now.

5-7  on left column = ask for help!

4 or less = your team is in real trouble. Call for help!

Paul R. Ford -1704 California NE, ABQ, NM 87110 – Phone/Fax  505-232-7900
*paul.ford@crmleaders.org*

# Appendix C

# Coaching on Gifts

### Spiritual Gifts: how are you powerful?

1. Using information and insight gained from all three parts of the gifts process (pp. 13, 15-16) in *Your Leadership Grip*, what probable gift combination do you have (top 3 or 4 gifts)? Some samples:

   - pastor-teacher — gift combination modeled in Ephesians 4:11

   - evangelist-apostle-teacher — the Apostle Paul's gift combo (1 Tim. 2:7)

2. People tend to understand their spiritual gifts most clearly through their gift liabilities. On pp 17-22 from *Your Leadership Grip*, determine whether or not the gift liabilities for each of your spiritual gifts fit you. Reminder: a gift liability is when you try to exercise a gift through your own strength instead of the Holy Spirit's power.

3. Most of us have gift combinations that blend together in unique ways. Because of this, learn to ask yourself and others the following questions:

   - With what gifts do you lead powerfully? The leadership gift or a combination of other gifts … pastoring and administration, or exhortation and administration, or evangelism and administration, etc.? (Note: what would be missing is the supernatural ability to originate vision.)

- With what gifts do you teach powerfully? The teaching gift or a combination of two other gifts that cause you to teach power-fully...exhortation and leadership, prophecy and leadership, exhortation and prophecy, exhortation and wisdom, etc?

- With what gifts do you preach powerfully? The prophecy gift or ...teaching and leadership, or exhortation and teaching, or evangelism and exhortation, or wisdom and leadership, etc?

- With what gifts do you pastor powerfully? The pastoring gift or a combination of exhortation and mercy, leadership and mercy, etc?

4. In the feedback that you have received from others, how many circles are on the top half (equipping gifts) and how many circles are on the bottom half (supporting gifts)? Does the top/bottom balance of circles reflect the same balance of your top four selected spiritual gifts? If not, you may have a misperception of your gifts. Make a sober estimate!

- All equipping gifts – designed exclusively to powerfully equip and release others to play their God-designed parts

- All supporting gifts – designed exclusively to powerfully serve and support others

- Combination of equipping and supporting gifts – designed with a combination that both equips and releases others, but also is able to serve and support others

# Appendix D

# Leadership Functions and Spiritual Gifts

*If you have one or more of the following leadership functions, you will commonly find one or more of these potential gifts in your gift mooshing.*

| Primary Leadership Function | Potential Spiritual Gifts |
| --- | --- |
| **Values Keeper** | administration<br>teacher<br>wisdom/word of wisdom<br>prophet<br>discernment of spirits |
| **Team Builder** | pastor<br>exhorter<br>leader<br>supporting gift: mercy |
| **Active Listener** | pastor<br>wisdom<br>exhorter<br>supporting gifts: helps, mercy<br>discernment of spirits |
| **Vision Sharer** | leadership<br>prophet<br>evangelist<br>exhorter<br>teacher |

**Equipping Releaser**

All equipping gifts:
exhorter
evangelist
leader
pastor
prophet
teacher
wisdom/word of wisdom
knowledge/word of knowledge

# Appendix E

# The Long and Unfinished Journey of Discovery at City on a Hill

## Pastor Dave Bruskas

### Overview

Most of our lessons have been learned through failure, not success. I am confident we are presently on the right path biblically and experientially. I also know we have not nearly yet arrived. Our journey is incomplete, but like most journeys, ours is best communicated in a series of shorter steps or phases.

### Phase One: Good News and Good Relationships in Symmetry

In the days before we knew what we were doing, evangelism happened organically and effectively as our people eagerly invited their friends, co-workers, family members, neighbors and strangers to join our new community large and small. It was really very simple. In those early days the small group and the large group were one and the same. We had one small group gathering weekly for the purpose of study, prayer, accountability and relationship. We also had a large group gathering weekly for worship in which the gospel was regularly proclaimed. The result was profound! Our seekers had the freedom to observe our community at study, prayer, fellowship and worship as they built growing friendships. They heard the message of reconciliation proclaimed as they experienced firsthand the ultimate apologetic, "By this will all men know you are my disciples, if you love one another."

*(John 13:35)* Then, came our greatest challenge: growth. The large group and the small group were no longer the same. We had to create several small groups to accommodate those participating in the larger group.

## Phase Two: Good News without the Good Relationships

Instinctively, we did what most churches do when faced with the reality of numerical growth. We emphasized our large gathering dispro-portionately to our smaller groups. We concluded that evangelism would happen mostly through the context of our large gathering. We removed most traces of outreach from the heart of our small groups. For the first time in our history, we came in contact with the church consumer. Growth continued. As a matter of fact, our larger group was larger than ever before. We had larger crowds and more money in the bank, but sadly, we were making very little impact in the lives of the spiritually lost of our city. Numerical growth and success according to our vision became inversely proportionate. The small groups we did have were anemic without the life-giving spiritual energy injected by new believers or serious seekers. People were no longer engaged in doing evangelism in the context of loving relationships (small groups). Any individual acts of evangelism were just that. Individuals were doing their best to reach lost people without the power of community behind them. They proclaimed the good news in one-on-one conversations with little relationship and even less affect. We saw many new members and very few converts. This led us to a dangerous overcorrection.

## Phase Three: Good Relationships without the Good News

It seemed to be a decision of common sense. If we were better off when we were smaller, then we should put the burden of evangelism on small groups. We would aggressively invite unbelievers to be in small groups. We would also de-emphasize the importance of proclamation in the large group setting. Although this new endeavor began with a fair amount of enthusiasm and intentionality, the results were unimpressive. Most groups quickly faded into holy huddles. Unbelievers were more leary of small group invitations than those to worship. The few who did come to faith were never assimilated into the larger body. We inadver-tently enabled the individualism we were trying to reverse. A common thread was: "Why be a part of the large group if I have all I need in my small group?" For the most part we lost our consumers as they balked at the call to small groups. We also lost what little impact we had previously, even in Phase Two. Unbelievers were loved, but the power of large group proclamation was lost. We saw fewer conversions than ever before. We also saw a decrease in lifestyle evangelism among our most active participants who were very discouraged by their lost friends declining invitations to small groups.

## Phase Four: Back to the Future

The power of the early church as stated powerfully in this chapter is found in all gifts being exercised through an incarnational community that utilizes gifts of proclamation and support alike. It is a community where everyone sees his or her role united in the process of communicating the good news in action and words through loving relationships. It is a single community in two dimensions: size (large and small) and function (relationship and proclamation). The invitation to community is not a choice between either/or, but, instead both/and. At City on a Hill, this means that all seekers are invited to engage in both dimensions of our community. Those who find their way to our community through a worship service are rapidly placed into healthy small groups. Those who enter through the door of small groups are challenged to be active in the larger group. We are presently in the beginning stages of rediscovery! In the brief period of time (4 months) since we equally stressed both dimensions, we have seen more conversions and more participation in our large and small group gatherings than ever before. We are now growing larger and smaller simultaneously.

# Other books by this author:

### Gift Discovery for Individual Leaders

*Your Leadership Grip* will help individuals assess their strengths and come to an understanding of where they need others to come alongside them. A Spiritual Gift assessment, Team Style questionnaire and the Primary Functions of Leadership assessment are all tools found in this book to help the readers make a sober estimate of who they are. (This book can also be paired with the Birkman Personality Profile for an added level of evaluation. Call 1-800-253.4276 for details and pricing.)

Retail: $10.00

### Team-Building Tools

*Discovering Your Ministry Identity* is designed to help teams/staffs understand each other and themselves. Learn to value the differences that make us strong together. The range of discovery covers the following categories:

- Spiritual Fitness
- Spiritual Gifting
- Ministry Burden
- Team Style
- Personal Values
- Leadership Strengths

Retail: $16.00

### Churchwide Gifts Implementation

*Unleash Your Church* will help your church implement a spiritual gifts discovery program. This comprehensive book will help you communicate biblical truths and principles of spiritual gifts as well as provide valuable information for a gift counselor, who can help place your people in the appropriate ministries for their giftedness.

Retail: $25.00